# SNOW TRAVEL
## Skills for Climbing, Hiking, and Moving Across Snow

MOUNTAINEERS
OUTDOOR EXPERT
series

# SNOW TRAVEL
## Skills for Climbing, Hiking, and Moving Across Snow

**Mike Zawaski**

THE MOUNTAINEERS BOOKS

**THE MOUNTAINEERS BOOKS**
is the nonprofit publishing arm of The Mountaineers,
an organization founded in 1906 and dedicated to the exploration,
preservation, and enjoyment of outdoor and wilderness areas.

1001 SW Klickitat Way, Suite 201, Seattle, WA 98134

First edition, 2012

Distributed in the United Kingdom by Cordee, www.cordee.co.uk

Manufactured in the United States of America

Copy Editor: Colin Chisholm
Cover and book design: The Mountaineers Books
Layout: Peggy Egerdahl
Illustrator: Mike Tea
Photographers: Mike Zawaski and Stacy Wolff unless otherwise noted

Cover photograph: *Colorado's Indian Peaks Wilderness*
Frontispiece: *Mount St. Helens, Washington*

*Library of Congress Cataloging-in-Publication Data*
Zawaski, Mike.
  Snow travel : skills for climbing, hiking, and moving across snow / by
Mike Zawaski.
       p. cm.
  Includes index.
  ISBN 978-1-59485-720-1 (pbk) — ISBN 978-1-59485-721-8 (ebook)
  1. Winter sports.  I. Title.
  GV841.Z38 2012
  796.9—dc23
                        2012036433

ISBN (paperback): 978-1-59485-720-1
ISBN (ebook): 978-1-59485-721-8

# Contents

**CHAPTER 4**

# Descending

**CHAPTER 5**

# Self-Arresting

**CHAPTER 6**

# Traversing, Resting, and Other Skills

## CHAPTER 7
## Hazards and How to Avoid Them

*When the snow conditions are good, your options for routes are endless.*

# Acknowledgments

This book would not have been possible without the help of many old and new friends who answered questions, shared perspectives, argued over seemingly trivial details, and went climbing with me. Thank you very much to Gus Alexandropoulos (*Gripped Magazine*); folks at the American Alpine Club Library; Aram Attarian (Outward Bound); Colorado Mountain School guides John Bicknell, Bob Chase, Bob Sharp, Mike Soucy and Eric Whewell; Luis Benitez; Chris and Jack Blees; Derek Branstrom; Robert Buswold; Josh Cole; Kathy Cosley; Chris Davenport (Kastle Skis); Susan Detweiler; John Dill and Mike Gauthier (Yosemite National Park); Rob Dillon; Austin Gibney (Never Summer Snowboards); Mike Hattrup (K2); Mark Houston; Jake Jones; Stephen Koch; Brian Lazar (Colorado Avalanche Information Center); Alexis Maget; Luke Miller; Mark Moore (Northwest Weather and Avalanche Center); Gary Neptune (Neptune Mountaineering); Black Diamond Equipment employees Bill Belcourt, Dave Mellon, and Kolin Powick; Virginia Rebélo; Dale Remsberg (American Mountain Guide Association); Christian Robertson; Billy Roos (Outward Bound); Tod Schimelpfenig (The Wilderness Medicine Institute of NOLS); Dan Shuteroff; Jared B. Spaulding; Hunter Waldron (K2); Jed Williamson (*Accidents in North American Mountaineering*); David "Heavy" Whalley; Jackson Wilson; and Joanne Yankovich. A special thank you goes out to Stacy Wolff for her great help taking photos, modeling for photos, and proofreading the book.

Thank you very much to the organizations that provided equipment and support for this book: Black Diamond Equipment, Camelbak, CAMP, Clifbar, Contour Cameras, Golite, Hotronics, Kastle Ski, K2, La Sportiva, Mammut, Ortovox, Outdoor Research, Petzl, Plum Bindings, Scarpa, Silva, Tech4O, and Voilé. I also want to thank all the folks at The Mountaineers Books, including Colin Chisholm, Mary Metz, and Kate Rogers.

# Introduction

*"If the only tool you have is a hammer, you see every problem as a nail."*
*—Abraham Maslow*

This book is intended as an introduction to the tools and techniques needed to travel safely over snowy terrain. Having the confidence and skill to climb and travel on snow opens the door to endless possibilities, allowing the adventurer to climb peaks or backcountry routes that in the summer might be unpleasant slopes of loose rock. Proficient snow travel not only opens up opportunities for climbing mountains but also lengthens the ski or snowboard season by a month or two. When snow and ice become your playground, hard-to-negotiate talus slopes and loose rock become obstacles you can avoid.

The following story is meant to illustrate the benefits of knowing how to travel safely over snow, and to inspire any reader to spend a few sunny summer days learning these fundamental mountaineering skills.

The Paintbrush and Cascade Canyon Loop in Grand Teton National Park is beautiful, but so popular in July and August that you might get turned away because the camping spots have all been taken. Park Service rangers are inclined to discourage hikers from attempting the route before the snow has melted entirely because, when the steepest portion of the trail up the pass is covered with snow, backpackers have fallen and slid into the boulders below. However, going in June is some people's only option, and going in the "off-season" has several advantages. Yes, you will miss most of the summer wildflowers, but fewer bugs, fewer people, and great snow are excellent incentives.

*The end of the rock is only the beginning of the fun.*

I once hiked up Paintbrush Canyon in the early season. Snow was plentiful, especially on the north-facing aspects of the canyon. The benefit of having a trail is that it makes finding the way easier and reduces hiker impacts. But when everyone walks on the same snow-covered trail, the snow gets compressed and freezes solid. So there we were, over a mile from the steep slopes on the pass, faced with the most difficult snow we would experience during the whole trip. So we pulled out our axes and proceeded to kick and chop steps as necessary. Safely beyond this steep section, we were left to find our own way as the trail was completely buried by snow. Our confidence on snow had allowed us to save time and to take an easier route, contouring along a 25-degree slope instead of hiking over slick rocks and trees that other hikers had used to avoid the snow.

The next day we encountered a mountain pass that would have been treacherous for an unprepared hiker. In the early morning the snow was firm and a set of tracks in the snow marked the trail. However, the tracks were melted out and the route, though low angle, crossed a steep section of snow with boulders below, an obvious hazard. My partner turned to me and said, "That looks like an accident waiting to happen." We instead opted for a shorter but steeper route, which had a safe runout in case my partner fell (i.e., there were no rocks to smash into). We also picked this steeper route because it faced more to the south, which allowed the snow to soften earlier so we could kick steps more easily. On our way down the other side of the pass, glissading and plunge stepping—where others had made riskier traverses while trying to stay on dry ground—was safer, faster, and more fun.

The information in this book summarizes my experience in the mountains but knowledge you gain from reading this text must be combined with knowledge based on your own experience in the mountains.

Climbing in a snowy environment requires that you continually stay present. Every step is a science experiment, and the result of each step is a new piece of data to consider. Predict the consistency of the snow and kick accordingly. Keep looking ahead and choose routes that seem best based on the information you have collected along the way. However, always be thinking of Plan B. Then when the snow you predicted to be firm turns out to be mush, you will already have an alternative in mind.

## ENVIRONMENTAL CONSIDERATIONS AND THE LEAVE NO TRACE (LNT) ETHIC

The alpine is a beautiful but fragile environment. If you are not already familiar with and invested in reducing your environmental impact, it is essential to improve your knowledge and skills before venturing up high where carelessness in the alpine environment has greater ramifications.

Soil, nutrients, water, and even sunlight can be scarce in the alpine. Plants

*Beautiful patches of flowers and other vegetation thrive in undisturbed places.*

must grow, flower, pollinate, and set seed between the time the last freeze occurs in early summer and the first freeze occurs in late summer. This may be only a month or so, depending on the year. Here are some key points to consider for each of the seven principles of Leave No Trace when traveling in snowy places.

**Plan Ahead and Prepare.** Planning for bad weather and darkness allows you to make choices that reduce your impact; for example, proper clothing and a headlamp helps you stay on the trail and avoid cutting switchbacks.

**Travel and Camp on Durable Surfaces.** In the spring and early summer, snow covers the trail in shady places and at higher elevations. Do your part to keep the trail narrow by staying on the trail. Walk through the muddy sections and kick steps through the snow instead of going around. Your boots will recover much faster than the plants trying to send up their first sprouts. When you have reached the top of your snow climb, spread your group out to avoid making any new trails in fragile soil, or walk together across snow and rocks until you get to a trail. Snow protects the soil underneath.

**Dispose of Waste Properly.** Because decomposition is incredibly slow above tree line, it is one of the worst places to bury solid human waste. The best technique is to relieve yourself at a lower elevation, pack things out, or hold it. Burying feces in the snow is a poor solution. When the snow melts it becomes "revenge of the feces" for the next climbers. It also transports water-borne parasites such as giardia.

**Leave what you find.** A common practice for people in the high country is to build rock cairns to indicate routes. Sometimes these can be useful because they concentrate heavy use or mark the way. Their usefulness decreases when trails of cairns exist all over the mountainside or when they provide no navigational benefit. Look for natural features as reference points.

Leave the rocks where you find them and leave the artwork to Mother Nature. That colorful crusty stuff on those rocks is alive. These lichens may be thousands of years old!

**Minimize Campfire Impacts.** Firewood is almost nonexistent in the alpine environment. The plants that grow there rely on the decomposition of other trees and plants for their nutrition. If you need to cook or boil water, bring a stove.

**Respect Wildlife.** Marmots, pikas, and pine martens are only a few of the amazing critters that live up high. Feeding wildlife damages their health, alters natural behaviors, and exposes them to predators and other dangers. In popular places marmots have become conditioned to hikers feeding them. As a result, marmots have become a nuisance and will destroy unattended gear to get to food. Also, respect closures so animals can raise their young in peace.

**Be Considerate of Other Visitors.** One great benefit of moving on snow is that you can find solitude and escape the crowds. If your descent takes you down a trail, hikers coming up have the right away. Step to the side and let them pass. This practice also avoids widening the trail.

For more information on the Leave No Trace ethic, visit www.LNT.org.

**A NOTE ABOUT SAFETY**

Safety is an important concern in all outdoor activities. No book can alert you to every hazard or anticipate the limitations of every reader. The descriptions of techniques and procedures in this book are intended to provide general information. This is not a complete text on snow travel technique. Nothing substitutes for formal instruction, routine practice, and plenty of experience. When you follow any of the procedures described here, you assume responsibility for your own safety. Use this book as a general guide to further information. Under normal conditions, excursions into the backcountry require attention to traffic, road and trail conditions, weather, terrain, the capabilities of your party, and other factors. Keeping informed on current conditions and exercising common sense are the keys to a safe, enjoyable outing.

*The Mountaineers Books*

# Chapter 1

*Climbing steep snowy peaks requires the right gear and the know-how to use it correctly.*

# Gear

*"The more knowledge you can put in your head,*
*the fewer things you have to put in your pack."*

Climbers today have more gear choices than ever. Equipment has been designed and made for a wide range of activities and for very specific uses, and the consumer must be careful to buy the right item for the intended activity. For example, some boots have crampons permanently screwed to them; they may be just the thing for some ice climbs, but you would never wear them all day on a peak climb.

The weight of your pack and gear is a common measuring stick for outdoor folks, but you might also challenge that notion by considering durability, usefulness, and safety. When purchasing equipment, consider application, durability, versatility, weight, and safety by asking yourself some important questions. How often do I plan to use it? What type of routes do I climb (or want to climb)? In some cases

gear has gotten lighter because it has been configured differently, but not necessarily better. Gear may be made lighter by using different materials, using less material, or becoming smaller. Thick leather boots kick steps better and last longer than nylon boots. Thinner pack material and clothing is lighter, but it wears out faster. Smaller carabiners and buckles may be just as strong as the older ones, but they may be nearly impossible to use with cold hands and big gloves.

On the other hand, lighter gear may allow you to hike farther and faster. A light piece of equipment is more enticing to carry and may come in handy. For example, a very light ice ax may be worth carrying during a summer backpack trip for that one snowfield that may or may not have melted out for the season.

Also consider that the gear you use on a regular basis for weekend climbing will receive far more abuse than the items you bring on a big trip. My mother knew better than to use her nice dishes for everyday eating at our house! Once you have purchased your gear, treat it well or it will wear out more quickly, be less functional, and less safe. Hitting your ax against rocks and walking through boulder fields with your crampons on will dramatically shorten their life no matter how good they are. Well-made gear, treated well, should last many years.

## DRESSING AND PACKING FOR SUCCESS

The battle to stay comfortable involves keeping your skin dry, and finding a balance between getting rid of extra heat quickly when you are working hard and saving your heat when you are not. Keep yourself comfortable by considering the ways you gain and lose heat, and adjust your actions accordingly.

Humans lose heat through the following four processes:

1. **Conduction:** The transfer of heat between objects through direct contact. Examples include standing on cold ground, having wet clothing against your skin, sitting on cold rock or snow, and exposing warm skin to cold air. Some materials conduct heat well and others poorly. Insulated clothing helps keep you warm because it traps air, which is a poor conductor, close to your skin. Rock and ice conduct heat about four times faster than snow. Aluminum and

steel conduct heat very well, which is why your feet feel colder wearing crampons and your hands get colder holding your ax. Wear dry clothing and reduce your contact time with items made of metal. Carry a small piece of ensolite to sit or stand on during long, cold stops, or just sit on your backpack.

2. **Convection:** Transferring heat by air or water molecules flowing across you increases conductive heat loss. Stay warmer by wearing windproof clothing and staying out of the wind.

3. **Radiation:** Energy is lost by emitting light (electromagnetic radiation). Every object on Earth emits some energy in the form of light; the type (wavelength) of light emitted depends on its temperature. Put a piece of metal in the fire long enough and its temperature will get high enough that it emits visible light. Human temperature is too low to emit visible light, but we are warm enough (even when we feel very cold) to emit infrared light. While it is impossible to reduce the energy we lose through radiating energy, we can wear layers of clothing that absorb this energy and radiate heat back toward our skin.

4. **Evaporation:** Heat loss that occurs when water changes from a liquid phase to a gas phase. Try this: blow on your dry hand. Notice how your hands still feels warm. Now, lick your hand and blow on the moist area; it will feel significantly colder. In fact, it takes 600 times more energy to evaporate a drop of water than it does to warm it up even 1 degree C (roughly 2 degrees F). This is why staying dry in a cold environment is so important for maintaining warmth. On the other hand, someone overheating cools off through evaporation very quickly when being fanned or standing in the wind while their skin is moist.

Humans gain heat through three processes:

1. **Metabolism:** Digesting food is a warming process for warm-blooded organisms. Continually snacking throughout the day helps fuel metabolism. Fats and proteins contain more calories per gram than carbohydrates, and they digest slower so they keep you warmer, especially at night when you are not exercising.

2. **Exercise:** The process of our muscles working generates heat.

3. **External sources:** Heat from outside the body. Examples include conduction by a heat pack, sitting on a warm rock, putting a hot water bottle in your jacket, or getting close to that special someone...or climbing partner while waiting out a storm. Radiative heat gain can come from standing in the sun or in front of a campfire. Convective heat gain is unlikely, but backcountry hot springs do exist!

Remember, putting on additional clothing or getting in your sleeping bag does not generate heat, it only contains it. It's the same principle as a thermos: hot chocolate stays warm and ice water stays cold in a thermos because the air between the contents and the outside world is a poor conductor.

Think of heat gain and loss as two sides of a scale. Your goal is to keep the scale balanced and to find that happy medium between preserving enough warmth to keep you comfortable and losing excess heat to prevent overheating. Leaving the trailhead wearing too many clothes and hiking fast may cause you to sweat profusely and, as a consequence, soak your insulating layers. If the wind is blowing where you stop to remove layers, you may become cold due to evaporative heat loss. If you then put your shell jacket back on, it will prevent your clothes from drying out and leave you with wet insulation all day.

## CLOTHING

There are two general rules to follow when it comes to layering for mountain travel. First, if you are warm before climbing, you are going to be overheating after you start. Second, it is easier to stay warm than to get warm.

Most climbs in the mountains involve long approach walks, and most of the time the steeper snow occurs at higher elevations and in exposed places where the temperatures are lower and the wind is stronger. Your layering combination should include layers of wool and synthetics (not cotton) against your skin and a shell layer on top to keep out the wind, rain, and snow.

On both the approach and the climb, you are typically generating excess heat. To keep yourself cool, leave your car or campsite with less clothing on than feels comfortable at first. A great piece of clothing is a hooded down or synthetic jacket that you can wear over other layers. Leave this on while you pack your pack and tie your boots; take it off and stuff it in your pack when you start moving. Keep yourself moving, but lose excess heat by taking off your hat, rolling up your shirt sleeves, untucking your shirt, and rolling up your pants to expose your calves. Base layers with a half-zipper in the front allow heat from your core to escape out around your neck. (This works best if you have bare skin exposed below.) Pit and side zips are useful when temperatures require you to wear a jacket or shell pants.

When traveling on snow where falling is a possibility, wear a helmet, sturdy hiking boots with gaiters, long pants, a long-sleeved shirt, and gloves. Snow crystals, even on a warm day, are amazingly sharp. Sliding down steep snow can cause painful abrasions to skin. Once you start to climb, changing layers may be difficult because a good stance may not exist. For this reason it is safer to wear extra insulation on your lower body and regulate temperature from your upper body in the same way you did on the approach.

Stay cool but keep your shell handy by putting it on and zipping it up only a quarter of the way. Now take your arms out of the sleeves and roll the jacket down; tie this consolidated package around your waist using the sleeves. With practice, you should be able to get your arms in and out of your sleeves while still wearing your pack.

Once you reach your high point and start descending, you are unlikely to generate the same amount of heat as you did during the ascent. Now is the time to put on more insulation, eat, and drink. If you plan to glissade, ski, or snowboard, wear proper clothing to protect your skin from abrasions on the snow. If you will be generating extra heat during your descent, postpone adding extra insulation. If your descent is prolonged or less energy intensive, dress accordingly.

### Gloves and Mittens

Your gloves will get wet on the snow, especially in summer. Gloves and mittens with removable liners will dry faster. They also allow you to wear only the shell or the liner, thus keeping the other half of the gloves dry. Always carry extra gloves. If it is cold out, bring warm mittens as well. To keep liners dry while wearing mittens, some people will put a bread bag between their shells and liners.

In really wet conditions, especially with above-freezing temperatures, get a pair of tough rubber gloves sold at fishing shops. Buy them a little big and wear thin fleece gloves underneath. Cinch them on your wrist with a rubber band. Avoid insulated rubber gloves because the insulation takes too long to dry inside the rubber shell.

Never set your gloves on the ground. They may get cold and wet, or be blown away or forgotten. Stuffing them into the front of your jacket keeps them warmer, but be careful that they do not fall out of the bottom of your jacket.

If you are not worried about your gloves getting cold, some gloves have a small loop sewn on the fingers that allows you to clip a carabiner to them so they hang with the fingers up to keep snow from falling in. "Idiot straps" (the strings that stick out of the trough of your gloves) keep you from dropping your gloves, but having your gloves dangling from your wrists can be awkward and with the opening of the gloves facing up, moisture can fall in.

### Gaiters

Snow will get in your boots unless you seal the tops of them in some way. Gaiters create a seal around the base of your boots and then cinch above your calf muscle to keep snow from sliding down into your boot. You may put them on over or under your pant legs.

Wearing gaiters over pants protects the pants from abrasion, moisture, and crampons. Wearing gaiters under your pant legs is advantageous for wet locations because rain will flow down the pants and drip off your legs instead of going between the pants and gaiters and into your boots. Some pants have grommets on either side of the cuffs so that an elastic cord can be tied through them and then stretched under your boot so your pants cover the tops of your boots. Gaiters form a better seal to keep snow out.

### Boots

Boots come in a seemingly endless array of styles and designs. When purchasing boots for climbing snow and peaks, consider these five variables: rigidity of the sole, stiffness of the upper boot, water repellency, durability, and warmth. Once you have found the type of boot that fits your needs, then consider weight.

The rigidity of the sole affects how easy it is to kick steps with your toe (front-pointing) in firm snow. Softer boots may allow you to kick steps with the sides of your feet, but front-pointing in firm snow may be impossible. Boots with a half shank are good for kicking steps; boots with a full shank do even better. The trade-off is that a rigid sole is less nimble for walking and scrambling. A full shank boot will accommodate all types of crampons, while a half shank will accommodate only select crampons.

The stiffness, water repellency, and durability is determined by the boot's material. Warmth is partially determined by the water repellency, but boots made for cold temperatures are insulated or have an insulated liner boot. A removable inner boot dries faster than the lining of an insulated boot.

Lightweight, nylon hiking boots tend to be very soft. These may be fine for climbing through soft, afternoon snow in the summer, but they would be a bad choice for a route that requires kicking steps in firm snow.

Plastic mountaineering boots (with a soft insulated liner) are durable, warm, and waterproof. They are excellent for kicking steps, but less nimble because of their rigid

sole and stiff upper boot. Snowboarders may choose boots like these over soft snowboard boots for climbing firm snow. Plastic boots and ski boots have rigid uppers that reduce the ankle articulation necessary for flat-footed climbing techniques with crampons. The rigidity of the sole does make kicking steps easier and less tiring.

### Helmet

A helmet is essential to protect your head from falling debris and to keep from hitting your head if you fall. If falling rock is a real hazard, keep your helmet on the entire time; removing your helmet to change hats or other clothing should be kept to a minimum. Wear your sunglasses (with a keeper string) over your helmet strap so you can take them on or off easily.

Be careful when you take your helmet off: Many helmets have slid away or been accidentally knocked off mountains. Set the helmet down with the opening of the helmet facing down. This "happy turtle" technique will dramatically reduce the chances of losing your helmet. Avoid damaging or losing your helmet by storing it inside your pack.

## PACKING FOR SUCCESS

Packing your pack well requires forethought about which items you are most likely to need. The less you carry on your back the easier and faster travel will be, but it is critical to carry enough to stay safe and comfortable in the backcountry. The Ten Essentials below are a good place to start, but you should evaluate how much of each item to bring before each outing.

## EATING AND DRINKING FOR SUCCESS

Both your muscles and your stomach require oxygen to work, one to contract and one to digest food. If you are climbing hard and you eat a large meal, both your muscles and your stomach will be deprived of some of the blood they require to do their job. Eating small amounts of food while climbing and during breaks is easier on the stomach. Carbohydrates provide quick energy, but because they are digested quickly their affect is short lived. Examples of carbohydrate-rich foods include fruits, energy bars, gels, and grains. Fats and proteins digest slower and provide longer-lasting energy; they also contain more calories per mass than carbohydrates. Thus, a pound of cheese has more calories than a pound of bagels. Make high-calorie foods accessible by storing them in a plastic bag in your jacket.

Staying hydrated in the mountains is critically important. The challenge while climbing during cold weather is to keep water accessible and above freezing. For more moderate temperatures, a Camelbak or other hydration system keeps your water accessible. Water bottles can be fitted with a strap and clipped to your pack or put in a handy nylon pouch.

In temperatures below freezing, an insulated Camelbak hose and nipple reduce the chances of your water freezing, especially if you blow air back into the hose after you drink. Some brands make insulated shoulder straps. However, Camelbak-type systems will freeze when your pack is off and your body heat is not keeping the water warm. On very cold days, water bottles should be carried in an insulated nylon pouch with the lid facing down; an alternative is to keep the bottle inside your jacket.

If you are running low on water, clean snow provides a safe water source. Snow falling from the sky is free of organisms that wreak havoc on our digestive systems because those parasites get into the water supply through fecal matter. Especially if the air is warm, keep your wide-mouth water bottle inside your shirt or jacket. After you take a sip, scoop up a sip worth of snow into your bottle, give your bottle a shake, and put it back into your clothing so the snow melts. Melting snow in your mouth is another option; it takes a lot of energy, but if hypothermia is not an issue the practice is safe.

Fresh snow is safest to consume, but if none exists use the cleanest, whitest snow you can find. Everyone knows to stay away from yellow or brown. "Watermelon snow" is the common name for an algae that lives on snow. You do not see it until around midsummer when snow accumulation for the year has ceased. Watermelon snow is easy to spot: The snow is orangish pink and even smells like watermelon but it is unsafe to drink.

While snow is inherently clean, the animals living in it are not. Beware of snow where alpine animals are active. Their scat may carry giardia and other bacteria. Water flowing from a snowfield or glacier should be treated.

### Ten Essentials

1. Navigation (map & compass)
2. Sun protection (sunglasses & sunscreen)
3. Insulation (extra clothing)
4. Illumination (headlamp/flashlight)
5. First-aid supplies
6. Fire (waterproof matches/lighter/candle)
7. Repair kit and tools
8. Nutrition (extra food)
9. Hydration (extra water)
10. Emergency shelter (tent/plastic tube tent/garbage bag)

Pack for success by carrying a backpack that is large enough to accommodate all your equipment, but not so big that it makes climbing cumbersome or adds significant weight. Make sure there is some way to attach your ice ax. Put the items you hope not to use (e.g., extra mittens, extra insulation) at the bottom of the main compartment. Stack additional items that you are more likely to need higher up. Remember to keep heavy items close to your back. While you might find a safe, flat spot on the rock or snow that allows you to dig into your pack and find that sandwich, the reality is that trying to take things out of your pack and keep them from falling down a slope is challenging and time-consuming. Even taking your pack off can be tricky and potentially dangerous if you slip. Reserve the top pocket of your pack for essential items. It may be easier to have your partner open your top pocket or dig into your main compartment and grab an item for you. To avoid wasting time fiddling with your things, have the essentials, including food, map or route description, slope meter/compass, and lip balm, easy to access in your jacket or pants pockets.

Leave your headphones at home. Even on the approach, it is important to have all your senses working. Things you may miss while wearing headphones include the "whumping" sound from settling snow, wind blowing high on the peaks, rocks tumbling down the valley walls, or that group just ahead of you. If you had heard them, you would have moved faster and reached the base of the climb first!

## THE ICE AX

An ice ax has four main uses: providing a point of balance while you travel, helping you self-arrest if you fall, acting as an artificial hold to help you climb upward, and acting as a tool for chopping steps or platforms into the snow.

Ice axes have been getting shorter, lighter, and more refined over the decades. Typically an ice ax is used for climbing snow, and an ice tool is for climbing ice (an ice pick is for making drinks!). Some ice axes today closely resemble the previous generation of ice tools. They are shorter, have a more aggressive pick for climbing ice, and may have a slightly bent shaft. The design of the modern ice tool has radically departed from previous designs. While you could use these for self-arresting, they are not for mountaineering because you cannot

*Photo 1-1. The parts of an ice ax*

plunge the shaft into the snow and some lack an adze or spike.

### CHOOSING AN ICE AX

An ax with an aluminum head and spike is designed only for climbing snow. An ax with a steel head and spike will perform better in snow but also perform well for climbing firm snow and ice. Choose an ice ax based on the following features (Photo 1-1):

**Head:** The head of the ax is made of either steel or aluminum and includes everything from the pick to the adze. Most heads are steel, but a few lightweight versions are an aluminum alloy. A steel head and spike will stay sharper longer. A heavier head penetrates farther in harder snow because you force more mass against the snow when you swing. A steel head is better for pounding in pickets and tent stakes, being pounded into the snow with another ax or rock, and for digging the occasional cat hole below tree line when nature calls. An aluminum head saves weight.

**Pick:** Modern pick shapes fit into two categories, classic and reverse curved. A reverse-curved pick will perform better when climbing water ice and alpine ice because it follows the arc of an arm swing and it is easier to disengage the pick from the ice when you lift up on the tool. A classically curved pick may perform better when used to self-arrest on very firm snow because it digs in more gradually, which allows you to stop more slowly. Teeth on the pick provide grip when climbing hard snow and when using your ax to hook rocks or tree branches. Your pick will become dull if it is hit or scraped against rocks.

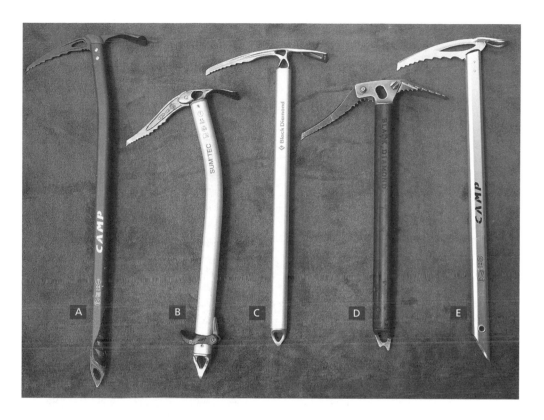

*Photo 1-2. (A) Traditional mountaineering ax; (B) Ax with reverse-curved pick, slightly bent shaft, and movable hand rest to make ice climbing easier; (C) Traditional ax with narrow portion at base of head is easier for people with smaller hands to use; (D) Traditional ice tool is heavier when used as an ax but is appropriate for snow climbing; (E) Lightweight ax with aluminum head and spike. Spikes decrease in effectiveness from left to right.*

**Adze:** The most important function of the adze is to chop steps or a platform into snow and ice. Sharp corners on the adze chop more efficiently than rounded ones. The adze may also be used to rest your hand on while climbing.

**Shaft:** The main difference between shafts is the shape. An essential function of the ax is to be plunged into the snow. A straight or slightly bent shaft accomplishes this best. A shaft that bends in multiple directions or has nonmovable protrusions for your fingers to rest on will never penetrate firm snow. A curved shaft prevents fingers from getting smashed when you are swinging the ax over your head on steeper snow or ice.

Some axes feature a rubber or plastic grip around the shaft, which provides insulation and helps you grip the shaft better. However a rubber grip is generally a disadvantage because it inhibits the shaft from plunging easily into firm snow.

With the invention of leashless ice climbing tools, manufacturers have added a small fixed protrusion that helps keep your hand from sliding down the shaft. This rest provides you greater grip with less energy expenditure when swinging the ax above your head on steep terrain. A new feature of hybrid ice axes that also serve as ice tools is a retractable or movable rest.

**Spike:** The primary job of the spike is to penetrate the snow or ice when you are climbing to give you better balance. Photo 1-2 shows a variety of spikes. Any spike will do when the snow is soft, but a sharp steel spike is essential when moving on firm snow. Your spike will dull over time if you use your ax as a walking stick on rocky terrain.

**Ratings:** A rating system has been developed by a European organization, the Comité Européan de Normalisation (CEN), that sets standards for some equipment. Axes can be given a B (basic) or T (technical) rating for the shaft and pick. The stress likely to be encountered during mountaineering activities fall within the B category. Ice tools designed for hooking rock and severe leveraging earn a T rating. Most ice axes have a B rating.

A pick with a T rating is one millimeter wider to accommodate the torqueing generated during mixed climbing. A shaft with a T rating can hold a greater perpendicular force, such as that encountered while levering with an ice tool during mixed climbing.

When purchasing an ice ax, start by considering the length and intended use. A longer ax will typically have a straight shaft and classically curved pick that cannot be changed out. Shorter axes feature either a classic style or a more technical style with the option of a slightly bent shaft and a reverse-curved pick, which may or may not be replaceable. (Needing to replace your pick is unlikely unless you regularly hit or hook rocks.)

### The Advantages of a Longer Ax

A longer ax is more effective at probing into the snow to assess the thickness of a snowbridge or the snow covering a void around rocks (see Chapter 7 for more on hazards). Bracing techniques are easier with a longer ax.

On low-angle slopes it can be awkward to use a short ax as a third point of balance, but if the angle is low you should not need your ax to support you unless it is very windy. A walking stick or trekking poles may be a better option for lower-angle terrain, but they add extra weight.

### The Advantages of a Shorter Ax

A shorter ax is better when you need to grip the base of the shaft and swing the pick above your head into the snow; though with good technique, a long ax works fine. A shorter ax is lighter. When plunging the shaft into deep snow on steep slopes, a shorter ax requires less energy because you do not need to lift your arm as high to remove the spike from the snow.

## CARING FOR AN ICE AX

Your ice ax is an important tool for keeping you safe. Treat it well by reducing its impact with rocks. Never just swing the pick or jab the spike into the ground; lay it down. A well-treated steel ax for climbing snow should rarely (once or twice a decade with high use) need sharpening.

If your ax does dull, use a flat file to sharpen it by placing the head on a solid surface, pushing the file away from you, and removing as little metal as possible. Filing the pick to a narrow point will make it more prone to dulling, but it will climb ice better. Never use an electric grinder because it generates too much heat, which can ruin the temper of the steel. Also, you may remove too much material.

## THE ICE AX LEASH

The goal of a leash, a strap connecting the ice ax to your wrist, is to help you avoid losing your ax while climbing. When deciding whether to use a leash, you should weigh the benefits and disadvantages.

Always having your hand through a loop of webbing and attached to your ice ax may sound logical, but this is not always the case. If you fall and drop your ax with a leash attached, chances are you will not regain hold of it. If you are tumbling, the chances increase for you to cut or impale yourself on the pick, adze, or spike if you are attached to the ax. Think of your leash as a tool to keep you from dropping your ax, not as a means of helping you regain a grip on it during a fall. Let this reality guide you in choosing when, if at all, to use a leash.

When ascending or descending, you will be switching the ax regularly between hands, and moving your hand in and out of the leash. This will slow you down and make you more prone to slipping.

There are situations during which having your hand through a leash is critically important. Traveling on a glacier is one of these, because dropping your ax if you fall into a crevasse will leave you helpless. Some climbers will clip their leash to their harness or the rope. This eliminates the hassle of moving your hand in and out of the leash as you switch hands on the ax. The disadvantage of this technique is that if you fall and drop your ax, you run a much higher risk of injury because the ax is attached so close to your midsection.

A leash is also advantageous when climbing steep snow and swinging the ice ax over your head. In this situation the leash tensioned around your wrist allows your wrist to hold a large fraction of your body weight and your fingers to control the shaft. When scrambling through mixed rock and snow, you may want to let go of your ax occasionally and have it dangle from your wrist while you grab the rock with your hands.

Remember, just because your leash is attached to your ax does not mean you need your hand through it. See Chapter 3, for techniques to quickly store your ax if you need both your hands for another purpose (e.g., scrambling on rock). You can also carry a leash in your pocket and easily attach it prior to encountering terrain where a leash is necessary.

Many commercial leashes exist (Photo 1-3, bottom). Leashes described as "full strength" hold up to 1500 pounds; others only hold up to 600 pounds. Choose one with a wrist loop into which your hand easily fits; the wrist loop should have a mechanism for cinching around your wrist. Some leashes and tethers are designed to connect the harness to the ax. Their purpose is to keep you from losing your ax; they are not meant for attaching yourself to an anchor or an ice ax in order to hang on them.

It is also possible to make your own leash (Photo 1-3, top). Tie a piece of $1/2$- or $9/16$-inch nylon webbing into a circle with a water knot. The loop is the correct size when it is girth hitched through the carabiner hole and the leash comes tight around

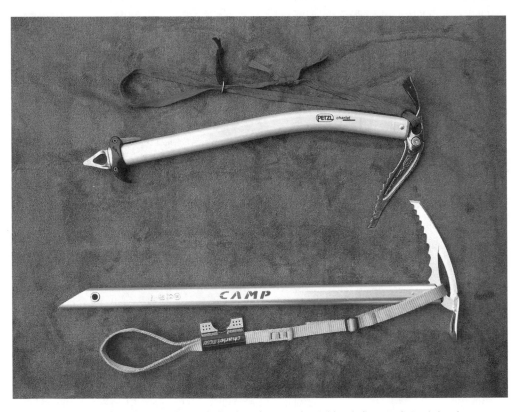

*Photo 1-3. Axes with a homemade leash (top) and a commercial leash (bottom). Both leashes are long enough to allow you to have your gloved hand through the loop and still grab the bottom of the shaft.*

your wrist when your hand is on the shaft just above the spike. To allow the loop to cinch around your wrist, slide a washer over the webbing. To make sliding the washer simple, tie a small loop of shoelace through the washer so you can slide it out of the way with your fingers or teeth. This option has some great advantages. The leash can easily be removed by undoing the girth hitch. The webbing is strong enough that it can be clipped to or removed to serve as part of an anchor system.

## CRAMPONS

Crampons are plates of metal with spikes (called points) that point down and outward. These plates strap or clip to your boots to give you traction on firm snow and ice. Crampons are an important tool to know how to use, but you do not need to get a pair before you venture out on snow. In fact, after becoming proficient kicking steps and using an ice ax, many people find no shortage of climbs and routes that can be done without crampons. Becoming proficient at kicking steps without crampons is essential. It will keep you from attempting to rely on crampons when you should not.

Having sharp spikes on your feet to provide traction may sound advantageous, but crampons should only be used on ice and firm snow where kicking steps is difficult or impossible. On these two mediums crampons provide excellent grip and require less energy to help your foot gain a secure purchase.

Climbers bring crampons year-round to glaciated mountains and places with permanent snow. Glaciated ranges such as the Cascades in the Pacific Northwest and the Alps in Europe are different than parts of the Rocky Mountains because under the yearly snowfall lies firn and glacial ice. Firn is snow that is older than one year but that has not yet turned to ice. It is very hard because it has gone through so many melt-freeze cycles that individual grains have morphed together. Glacial ice and firn are found on glaciers and permanent snowfields late in the season or in places where the wind has stripped away the fresh snow. The Coastal Ranges (e.g., Sierra and Cascades) of the United States receive wetter snow and have higher temperatures than ranges in the interior so their snow has more melt-freeze cycles to increase its density. These ranges also receive rain during any season, which can freeze soon after and solidify the snow.

On mountains without permanent snow or glaciers, the snow is never more than one year old. This prevents the snow from metamorphosing for multiple years (which would increase its density and make it more difficult to kick steps in). Climbing nonglaciated peaks without crampons during the summer is very common. Crampons come in handy most when climbing snow that is in the shade after a cold night. Overall, crampons are usually not necessary on most nonglaciated routes in the lower forty-eight states, but you never know when they may be useful. Bring crampons to travel on a glacier, to climb snow that has survived past August, to climb shaded routes up the north side of mountains, and to climb narrow gullies where flowing water may freeze to ice.

## CHOOSING THE RIGHT CRAMPONS

Mountaineering crampons come in three basic varieties. Aluminum models are for walking and climbing on hard snow; they are not for climbing ice because the metal is too soft, but they are often used by climbers and ski mountaineers looking to save weight. They weigh approximately half as much as steel versions. Steel models with horizontal front points are the most versatile because they work well on snow and ice. Steel will remain sharper longer, especially when used for climbing and scrambling over rocks. The third type, used for ice and mixed climbing, is also made of steel but the front points are vertical. A narrow (vertical) front point has less surface area to help it grip snow. Hybrid versions of these front points (narrow in the front for ice and rock, and wider near the back to help in snow) are sold with some crampons.

In the past, crampons were defined as rigid, semirigid, and hinged. Rigid models had a steel frame with no flex (a popular model was called Foot Fangs). Hinged crampons had an actual hinge that engaged when your boot flexed. Modern technology employs a spring steel bar to connect the front and rear sections of the crampons, which makes the crampons either semirigid or flexible for hiking boots and snowboarding boots.

Before you purchase crampons, make sure you have rigid boots, and that the binding style of the crampons you choose is compatible with your boots. Crampon bindings come in three basic styles.

The most universally accommodating system is the strap on (Photo 1-4A), which has evolved over the years and become much easier to use than earlier incarnations. The universal component is a strap-on binding system that fits almost any mountaineering boot. Strap-on crampons do not typically fit over the front protrusion on ski boots, however. Because snowboarding boots tend to have a wider toe, companies make modified crampons for these boots.

The most common rigid binding design, called the step-in, has a bail in the front to fit over a boot's toe welt, and a levered bail in the rear to snap over a boot's heel (Photo 1-4C). These work best for rigid boots with heel and toe welts, and they provide a secure and precise fit. They tend to work well with both mountaineering and ski boots, including telemark boots.

A third type of crampon binding, called the pneumatic or Scottish style, employs a combination binding with a levered bail in the heel and a strap system over the toe (Photo 1-4B). These are for semirigid boots with a heel welt. Crampons with a heel bail are faster to put on and remove. A horizontal front point, steel crampon with a combination binding may be the best choice for mountaineering. Most boots designed for some level of mountaineering will have a heel welt.

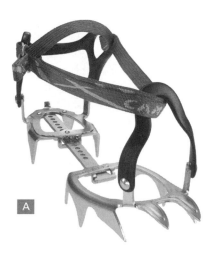

*Photo 1-4:*

*(A) Aluminum crampons with strap-on bindings*

*(B) Steel mountaineering crampons with a pneumatic or Scottish-style binding*

*(C) Steel crampons with vertical front points for ice climbing with a step-in binding.*

*Different crampon types can be purchased with different binding configurations. Note the anti-balling plates on the styles shown in B and C.*

Many crampons today come equipped with anti-balling plates, which are rubber or plastic plates that mount on the crampons and prevent soft, warm snow (the sort that's good for making snowballs) from accumulating on the bottom of your foot. These clumps of snow can become so large that the points of your crampons cannot touch the snow and you lose traction. Aftermarket anti-balling plates are available.

Crampons for lightweight hiking boots and running shoes are referred to as traction devices. Most of these resemble chains for car tires, and many people use them for running and hiking on icy trails. A couple of these designs resemble mountaineering crampons, but they lack front points. Manufacturers warn you that these are not for technical climbing. They are designed to flex with soft-soled boots or shoes. For climbing peaks, sturdy boots and knowing how to kick steps will eliminate the need for these devices in most situations. For mountaineering, true crampons are superior.

## SKI POLES AND TREKKING POLES

For skiers, split-board snowboarders, and snowshoers, ski poles are essential. They provide balance and an effective means by which to propel yourself forward over snow.

Ski poles or walking sticks are also helpful for climbers approaching or descending from a snow climb, especially when soft snow is likely. Sectional, expandable poles are available; they collapse to a convenient size for strapping to your backpack when not in use. Alternatives to poles include make-shift walking sticks such as tree branches you may find lying on the ground. Another option is to attach the ice ax to a short piece of ski pole using hose clamps. When the steeper climbing begins, the short section of pole can be stashed in your backpack.

Another tool designed for skiers but useful for mountaineering as well is a ski pole with an ice ax pick attached to the ski pole grip. The most popular version is the Black Diamond Whippet. The Whippet works as regular ski pole most of the time, but in the event of a fall the skier has the pick in hand for self-arresting (Photo 1-5). Ski mountaineers also use the Whippet as a lightweight ice ax when they are climbing steep slopes while carrying skis on their backs. Like any of the sharp, pointy things discussed in this book, the self-arrest pole should be used with caution. The sharp pick extending from the grip can cause severe penetrating trauma. The Whippet is not an ice ax, and without an adze it is ineffective for cutting steps. It is not meant to be swung over your head like an ice ax on steep snow or ice.

*Photo 1-5. A climber demonstrates the correct way to hold the Whippet for self-arrest (see Chapter 5).*

Photo 1-6. An avalanche beacon should always be worn correctly, never carried in your pocket, and each climber should have a probe and shovel to assist with a rescue.

## AVALANCHE EQUIPMENT

If you plan to climb or descend potential avalanche slopes (slopes greater than 30 degrees) or an avalanche runout zone, you and your partners need to bring the right avalanche gear and know how to use it. Always wear an avalanche beacon and carry a shovel, an avalanche probe, and a first-aid kit. Always wear your beacon close to your body so that, even if you are buried, the beacon stays with you. Clothing and packs can be torn off during an avalanche; never carry your beacon in a pocket or pack.

Proper instruction and practice are essential to using avalanche equipment effectively. When a victim is buried, chances of survival are very limited, especially after the critical first fifteen minutes have passed. Other rescuers may not be available, so your life, or the life of your friend, may be in the hands of those at the scene. (See Chapter 7 for further avalanche safety information.)

# Chapter 2

A climber front-points up the Dragon's Tail Couloir in Rocky Mountain National Park using the low dagger technique with his right hand and holding a Black Diamond Whippet in his left.

# Getting Started: Ascending

*"Learning is not a spectator sport."*

Before getting into the finer points of climbing snow, it is important to see the big picture. Unlike rock climbing, where the number and quality of hand and footholds is fixed, improving your steps and manufacturing protection placements is what snow climbing is all about. Falling while rock or ice climbing often has serious consequences, which is why people use ropes. On snow slopes climbers normally travel without ropes. This is due partly to the terrain itself, but also to the many options available for protection and for climbers to modify the snow to make it easier to climb. Stay safe by following this progression of ways to protect yourself while climbing.

1. Choose the correct technique for your feet and kick good steps. Good footwork is your first and most important line of security. Use your ax for balance only, not to hold your weight.

2. When your steps feel less secure (or the consequences of falling increase), use your ax as a third point of security by either jabbing the pick or the spike into the snow using one of the techniques outlined in Chapter 3, Using Your Ice Ax. Drive the pick or spike deep into the snow and keep a good grip so that if you slip, your upper body and ax prevent you from sliding.

3. When it becomes too difficult to kick steps, put on crampons. Use your ax as a point of balance or for support.

4. If crampons are not an option, or the section of firm snow is short, cut steps with your ice ax.

5. If your feet are sinking deeply and your ax is not able to gain purchase in unconsolidated snow on a steep slope, your primary concern may be an avalanche. Move to firmer (and preferably lower-angle) snow immediately.

6. If the area of snow you are attempting to cross is steeper than you are comfortable with and you do not have crampons, descend and find a different route. If some but not all members of your group feel uncomfortable climbing the slope, one option is to have those members belayed up the slope by a person who has climbed ahead and created an anchor.

7. Long, steep sections of frozen snow and ice usually require roped climbing techniques. If you have experience lead climbing, using a rope and lead climbing while you place protection in the snow and rocks is an option. Covering this skill is outside the scope of this book.

The previous skills should be used in a progression because employing a technique too early may slow you down and possibly make you less safe. For example, in soft snow on a low-angle slope you should be able to kick adequate steps and feel secure without needing to drive the entire shaft of your ax into the snow with each step. Using your ax in this manner is tiring, will slow you down, and may expose you to hazards higher on the mountain that would not have been an issue if you had reached the summit earlier in the day.

Good risk management involves considering both the probability and

## CLIMBING AS A ROPED TEAM—GOOD OR BAD IDEA?

A common error made by climbing groups has been to create a roped team, where members tie into the rope at even intervals and ascend/descend in a straight line. History has shown that a rope team that includes inexperienced climbers is likely to end in disaster if any members (especially the highest climber) fall and fail to self-arrest. During roped team travel, there is always the risk that a fallen climber will pull the other climbers off their feet and into an uncontrolled slide.

Two tragic examples of this occurred on glaciated peaks: on Ptarmigan Peak in Alaska in 1997 and on Mount Hood in Oregon in 2002. In both situations a member of a roped team fell and failed to self-arrest, pulling the other members down the slope. These situations became even worse when other roped teams climbing below were knocked down the mountain by the sliding teams. These giant tangles of ropes, axes, and people stopped only when they collided with a boulder field or fell into a crevasse after sliding hundreds of feet. Major injuries and fatalities occurred.

On a glacier, climbing as a roped team is a mandatory activity due to crevasse danger. A climber falling into a crevasse typically generates much less force on the other climbers than a climber sliding down a snow slope because the effect of the rope cutting into the snow over the lip of a crevasse increases the friction and decreases the acceleration of the falling climber.

Roping up on a steep slope is not recommended for beginning climbers or teams traveling in steep terrain with inexperienced members. If you are hoping to climb glaciated peaks, seek further instruction on roped travel and running belays. For steep slopes, consider belaying inexperienced climbers.

consequences of an accident. The probability means how likely a fall or other accident is; the consequences are the events following an accident. When you are just learning, the probability of falling is high, so you practice in a safe location where the consequences of falling are low. As you climb steeper slopes and bigger mountains, the consequences of falling will increase. To manage this risk you will need to improve your skills and employ many of the techniques listed above for protecting yourself.

This is how experienced climbers climb big mountains: by being fit, by continually improving their skills, by making good choices, and by practicing effective risk management.

## SLOPE RATINGS AND DIFFICULTY LEVELS

This book avoids providing any numerical rating system or comparative rating system (e.g., slope X will be harder to climb than slope Y) because no standardized system has been created for rating snow climbs. Slope angle is only one variable in determining the difficulty of a route and the conditions of snow vary dramatically. For example, ascending a 5-degree slope of frozen water without crampons may be more difficult than climbing a 50-degree snow slope.

Unlike rock, which rarely changes, the texture of the snow may (and usually does) vary dramatically during a single day, during a single season, and over the years. This is an important concept to remember when consulting guidebooks or other sources of information about the difficulty of a route. Slope angle is commonly used in guidebooks to describe difficulty. It is likely to be consistent with what is written in a guidebook (if the author measured it correctly), but a few important variations may exist. Early in the spring the snow may be difficult to climb because it is poorly consolidated; this makes kicking steps and self-arresting more difficult. Recent snowfall can also dramatically change the route. Cornices may last well into the summer and may be much larger or smaller than "normal," making the last few meters of a route difficult or impassable.

As melting continues during the climbing season, sections of snow may melt out completely, requiring some rock climbing. Large gaps between the snow and the rock walls may make transitioning between the two impossible. If you are climbing a route from a glacier, the snowbridge covering the moat or bergschrund may have melted, preventing you from even getting on the route.

## THE FALL LINE

The fall line is the path an object will take if rolling or sliding down a slope. If the slope is featureless, the fall line will be straight down. However, slopes commonly contain concave and convex sections that funnel or divert falling objects respectively. No matter what medium you are climbing (snow, ice, or rock), knowing the fall line below you is essential because it tells you where you will slide if you fall and where any rocks or ice you dislodge will go (e.g., onto your partner below you). Assessing the trajectory of snow or rocks falling from above can help you choose a safe route or resting place.

As you gain experience climbing, you should be able to look down a slope and identify the fall line. You can assess the fall line by rolling a snowball down the slope to see where it goes. While moving in the mountains you should continually assess which direction you would fall if you slipped and whether there are any hazards above or below you. As you climb, spend as little time as possible in the center of a gully (often called the bowling alley); it is typically the fall line of hazards above. For gullies that take a diagonal path, stay to the uphill side because debris will funnel to the downhill side.

When glissading down a snow slope, understanding the fall line will help you determine your path and avoid hazards. Remember, unless you are on a snow slope that goes straight up or down the mountain and has a concave trough down the middle, your fall line is going to angle left, right, or in multiple directions.

*Photo 2-1. Snow bouldering next to a large boulder is a great way to improve your skills for climbing steep snow.*

## IMPROVING YOUR SKILLS WITH MINIMAL RISK OF INJURY

Consider improving your snow climbing skills the same way you improved your rock or ice climbing skills. Find a snow "cliff" at the base of a mountain where you can set up a top rope or do some snow "bouldering" in a location with a safe runout and no avalanche or rockfall danger above.

Short but steep sections of snow commonly form in the late spring and early summer near large boulders and at the base of rock walls when the heat from the rocks melts out a large pocket of snow around it. These features may last well into the fall season when the snow becomes very firm. If using a top rope, set your anchor at least five feet back from the edge so you can safely practice climbing over the lip.

Practice climbing up and down without an ice ax, with one ice ax, and with two ice axes. In the fall (and occasionally in the summer when the snow freezes solid), practice the same skills but with crampons as well. Practice cutting steps up and down.

## DAILY AND SEASONAL CHANGES IN THE SNOWPACK

Planning a successful and safe climb means understanding how the snowpack changes daily and throughout the year. To understand and make some predictions about the firmness of the snow, a few scientific principles must be understood. The first is that light is more than just the visible light colors of the rainbow, and comprises the entire electromagnetic spectrum. Gamma rays, x-rays, ultraviolet (UV), visible, infrared (IR), and radio waves are all types of light, differentiated by their wavelength and frequency; they all travel at the speed of light.

The second important concept is that all objects emit light. The type, or wavelength, emitted is dependent upon the temperature of the medium. Humans, the earth, and clouds, because of their temperature, emit infrared (IR) light. You have seen IR light if you have used or seen footage from a night vision camera. The higher the temperature, the shorter the wavelength emitted. When you first start your camp stove, it is cold and emits minimal infrared light, but after burning gas for 20 minutes it turns red and emits visible light. The sun emits mostly visible light. A warmer object will not only emit a different wavelength than a cooler object but will also emit much more energy.

The third important concept is that different materials absorb or reflect different amounts of light. Dark objects (e.g., rocks, trees) absorb more visible light than light-colored objects (e.g., clouds and snow). *Albedo* is the term used to describe a material's reflectivity. Fresh snow has an albedo of about 0.9; it reflects 90 percent of the visible light that hits it. Dirty, darker colored snow from late summer (albedo of 0.3) reflects only 30 percent; this means it absorbs about 70 percent of the sunlight hitting it. Snow absorbs almost 100 percent of the IR light hitting it. Tree wells (depressions in the snow that form around trees) and elephant traps (see Chapter 7) form because warm trees and rocks radiate IR energy into the snow and melt it.

To further understand the snowpack it helps to understand the changes that come about from the earth orbiting the sun with a tilted rotational axis. During the summertime in the Northern Hemisphere the sun rises north of east and sets north of west. This means the sun spends more than 12 hours above the horizon warming the surface and less than 12 hours below the horizon allowing the surface to cool. The other consequence is that when the sun is north of east or north of west, it shines on slopes with a north-facing aspect. Additionally, the sun is higher in the sky in the summer than in the winter. The sun never gets directly overhead at latitudes higher than the tropics (plus and minus 23.5 degrees latitude). When the sun is higher in the sky, a region of the earth receives more energy than when the sun is lower in the sky (Figure 2-1). On the other hand, a single landform such as the steep, east-facing slope of a mountain may get its most intense sunlight in the early morning

*Figure 2-1. The range of heights of the sun at noon (at 40 degrees north latitude on the summer and winter solstices). The sun is much higher on the sky at the summer solstice (June 21) and so shines over the top of the mountain; all sides of the mountain receive some solar radiation each day. The winter solstice sun (December 21), on the other hand, is much lower at noon so even south-facing slopes receive minimal sunlight; steep north-facing slopes receive no solar energy in midwinter.*

## THE REASONS FOR SEASONS

There is a common misconception that summer is warmer because the earth is closer to the sun. However, the shape of the earth's orbit is nearly circular, which means the earth is approximately the same distance from the sun all year; in fact, the earth is closest to the sun in January. The earth experiences seasons because its axis is tilted. As a result of this tilted axis, the angle of the sun's rays hitting a hemisphere and the hours of daylight that hemisphere experiences vary throughout the year. The seasons progress slowly because the changes described above are minimal on a day-to-day basis.

hours when the sun is low in the sky but shining directly on that face. When the sun is higher in the sky it shines over the tops of mountains and onto north-facing slopes that are in the shadows during the winter.

Winter in the Northern Hemisphere is characterized by a sun that rises south of east and sets south of west giving us less than 12 hours of sunlight to warm the earth and more than 12 hours of darkness, allowing the earth to cool down more than it heats up. The sun also never gets as high in the sky in the Northern Hemisphere so the earth receives less intense radiation. Due to these factors, northerly facing slopes receive minimal, if any, solar radiation.

During the winter the ground is covered by fresh, highly reflective snow, the sun is low in the sky and up for a minimal amount of time; so the mountains are cold and the snow stays more powdery and sticks together less. Less is, of course, a relative term. The sun does shine, melting and altering the surface of the snowpack. In addition, wind, avalanches, and gravity act to cause compaction of the snow. For the aforementioned reasons you will find

hard-packed snow in winter, but mostly on south-facing slopes and areas exposed to strong wind. The snow on the north side of a mountain stays powdery longer because it receives minimal solar energy. This is where powder seekers go to find good snow long after winter storms.

The coastal ranges of the United States receive much wetter snow and have warmer winter temperatures than ranges in the interior (such as those in Colorado, Utah, Wyoming, Idaho, and Montana). On the West Coast a big storm will bring lots of wet snow, which people refer to as "Sierra cement" and "Cascade concrete." Warmer winter temperatures help the snow settle faster and release water into the snowpack, which then freezes solid on colder days. This is why people wear crampons more in the Pacific Northwest. In the interior ranges much of the moisture from storms that originate in the Pacific Ocean has been lost on the way to Utah and Colorado so the snow is lighter. Consistently colder temperatures in these mountains keep the snow colder and reduce its compaction. When the time between storms is prolonged, the snow surface is exposed to the sun and wind longer, causing the snow grains to metamorphose and freeze together, thus forming a sun or wind crust. If the wind is the more dominant force, it will differentially erode and metamorphose the snow, sculpting it into intricate patterns called *sastrugi*.

As the earth continues in its orbit toward springtime, the sun is out for more hours and is higher in the sky, which causes more snow to melt. With more of the dark-colored landscape exposed because of melted snow or winds having blown the snow away, the ground begins to heat up. The sun rises farther north along the eastern horizon (and sets farther north along the western horizon) each day and its height at noon increases; therefore, more of a mountain receives direct solar energy. As summer approaches, the snow melts away first in the low valleys, which may make you wonder why you are walking up a dry valley with skis or a snowboard on your back, but you may be rewarded when you find yourself skinning up the low-angled section of the valley where others are postholing. Slopes with a more southerly aspect will become firmer before northerly slopes because they receive more solar energy.

The summer snowpack is in a daily melt-freeze cycle wherein the snow temperature drops below freezing at night and gets above freezing during the day. This is when the snow climbing season starts getting good. If you plan to ski or snowboard in the high country, early summer is a great time. Avalanches still occur in early summer so descending on snow is safer

earlier in the day. On nights when the air temperature is above freezing (especially if it's cloudy), the snow may be soft and easy to climb even in the early morning. The snow is typically hardest around dawn when the temperature is lowest. The best weather conditions for a hard freeze occur after a clear night with minimal wind. This is the time of year for getting up really early so you can avoid postholing through the soft snow in the valley. One reason the snow stays soft is because the trees emit IR light at night, keeping the air temperature higher. The other reason is that the trees shade the snow from the sunlight, reducing compaction. Slopes that face south, east, and northeast soften first so they require an extra early start. West- and northwest-facing slopes soften later in the day. Slopes that face north receive some solar energy, but not much; therefore the snow stays harder in the morning and all throughout the day. North-facing slopes take longer to consolidate in the spring, but they keep their snow longer in the summer, possibly all year.

Without new snow the surface of the snow becomes pitted with depressions and grooves, making skiing and snowboarding difficult and potentially dangerous. Snow riders looking to extend their season the most will seek north-facing slopes in the summer after the south-facing slopes have formed grooves and sun cups.

As summer comes to a close the snow disappears from all but a few places. These permanent snowfields, glaciers, and shaded gullies have very different climbing conditions in the fall. Repeated freezing and

**TERMS USED TO DESCRIBE SNOW**

**alpine ice and water ice:** Alpine ice is the result of snow that has undergone so many melt-freeze cycles that once individual grains have morphed into a nearly coherent mass of ice. Water ice forms when liquid water freezes (e.g., a frozen waterfall).

**corn snow:** Large, rounded snow and ice grains that form after many melt-freeze cycles. Corn snow freezes overnight, then softens in the sun. This snow is a favorite of skiers and boarders in the spring and summer.

**firn:** Snow that is more than one year old. The transitional state between snow and glacial ice.

**névé:** Climbers use the term to describe snow that is firm or Styrofoam-like, into which your crampons penetrate and stick well. Geologically, firn and névé are the same.

**sastrugi:** Intricate patterns formed by the wind as it scours the surface snow. Sastrugi may or may not provide a firm surface for climbing.

**sun crust:** A hard crust of snow that forms when snow is melted by sunlight and refrozen. Sun crusts form most on south-facing slopes. When a crust is buried by new snow, it provides a sliding surface for slabs of snow that develop above it, causing dangerous avalanche conditions. These layers can also be challenging for people traveling across them with skis and skins because neither skins nor edges will grip.

**sun cup:** Depressions in the snow caused by the differential "erosion" of the snow by sunlight or warm winds. They begin forming in late spring and make skiing and glissading difficult. Their concave shape makes climbing easier.

thawing of the snowpack converts snow into something closer to ice. Late season snow may still be soft enough to travel over without crampons, but usually only in rigid boots. In shady places and on longer routes, slipping and falling on this late-season snowpack will have severe consequences; wearing crampons helps prevent falls. Glaciated peaks will have the least amount of fresh snow covering the firn and ice, making crampons mandatory.

Two common challenges for climbers occur when snowfall begins in the early winter. Where any previous snow has entirely melted, a new layer of snow on top of a boulder field means you have to be careful to avoid slipping or twisting a joint while stepping between boulders. Travel through these areas is easier without crampons. Once you get off the rock, you may find snow of two very different consistencies. On the surface or in protected areas there may be fresh, unconsolidated, or wind-packed snow. Underneath this snow there may be ice. Kicking crampons into the ice or deep snow is

## TECHNIQUES FOR YOUR FEET
### (*PIED* IN FRENCH)

The following table lists the French and English terms for the most common foot techniques. It starts with the techniques used on flatter terrain and progresses to those you would use as the slope gets steeper. All of the following techniques can be used with or without crampons except the French technique.

| NAME: FRENCH | NAME: ENGLISH | |
|---|---|---|
| *Pied marché* (pronounced: PEE-ay marsh-ay) | Walking technique | |
| *Pied en canard* (pronounced: PEE-ay en cah-nahr) | Duck step | |
| N/A | Sidestepping | |

*Table 1-1*

## TECHNIQUES FOR YOUR FEET (CONTINUED)

| NAME: FRENCH | NAME: ENGLISH | |
|---|---|---|
| *Pied à plat*<br>(pronounced:<br>PEE-ay ah plah) | French technique | |
| *Pied troisième*<br>(pronounced:<br>PEE-ay trua AH-zee-emm) | Three o'clock,<br>combination<br>technique, or<br>American technique | |
| N/A | Front-pointing,<br>German technique | |

straightforward, but caution is required when you expect the snow to be deep and unconsolidated but you find instead a thin layer of powder covering the ice. It is usually safer to kick more aggressively than to kick softly and slip.

The winter avalanche season begins when new snow falls, sometimes bonding poorly to the firm snow remaining from the previous year. Deaths from avalanches occur even in October. Winter ascents of mountains require a solid understanding of avalanches, avalanche gear, and winter modes of travel (i.e., skis or snowshoes). During winter the best place to find hard snow for walking is on areas that receive strong wind and direct sunlight.

## CLIMBING TECHNIQUES

Techniques for kicking steps and using an ice ax originated mostly in Europe, and the names of the techniques tend to be of French origin. Over time, English translations and more descriptive titles have also evolved. In reality, there is no simple set of climbing terms in English that translate to the terms in French. This is partially because different techniques are not always used in isolation; they are blended with others to create new techniques. This book uses a descriptive approach and includes the French terms that North Americans commonly use. All the terms commonly used will be mentioned, but to keep things simple, each technique will be referred to using only one name.

The French system for naming a technique begins with telling you whether this technique is for your feet or your ax. The French word for *ice ax* is *piolet*. Techniques involving your ax are preceded by this word. Techniques for the feet are preceded by the word *pied*, which means *foot*. See Tables 2-1 and 3-1.

## THE BASICS OF KICKING STEPS

Kicking good steps is your primary mode of protection when climbing snow and arguably the most important skill presented in this book. Kicking steps means using your boots, without crampons, to create small platforms for your feet to rest on. The decision-making process for deciding which step to use can be summarized in two sentences:

1. Use the least amount of energy to kick your steps, but also use the right step to stay stable enough to avoid falling.
2. Follow the shortest path along your route, but balance this by choosing a safe route and not tiring yourself out.

The following techniques for using your feet to ascend have no hierarchy. Walking technique, sidestepping, front-pointing, and duck step are the four basic steps. Some variations are included, but these steps are not mutually exclusive; they blend together. As you become more proficient, you will see how the walking technique merges with any of the next three. Front-pointing blends with the duck step, then becomes a sidestep. You will also choose the right step for one foot independently of what the other is doing. Continually pay attention as you climb to determine if a particular step is (or was) correct for your situation.

There are two basic approaches to kicking steps. On softer snow, kick your level foot into the snow, creating a cavity for you to stand in. This is easier if you are wearing rigid-soled boots. The second approach, and the one requiring the best technique, is to kick (or saw) a small platform for the sole of your boot to rest on. Your goal with each kick is to create a platform that has enough surface area so that you feel comfortable standing on it. How much of your boot edge should rest on the snow is personal preference. On firm snow with rigid boots experienced climbers may cut an area only a centimeter deep; less experienced climbers will want a larger step. In softer snow, it is probably best to have at least a quarter to a third of the surface area of your boot on the platform.

To make sense of why some techniques may work better than others for kicking steps, it is worth considering how snow or other mediums behave when you hit them. Consider these examples that may be closer to home. Why is it easier to split a round of wood by axing it closer to the edge than in the middle? Why is it easier to break apart a slab of ice on the sidewalk when you start from the edge than the center? The answer is that all these materials split more easily when you provide a location for the broken material to go; and being near the edge requires a smaller amount of material to be broken in order to completely separate

it from the main body. This is why kicking steps is easier when the snow is featured and also why you swing your foot into the slope at an angle (sidestepping or duck stepping—see below) instead of kicking straight into the snow when front-pointing; the snow you kick can be dislodged from the slope instead of being compressed into the slope.

Apply these fundamentals when kicking steps:

- Swing your leg more from the knee than the hip.
- Kick like you mean it! Firm snow is not for tiptoeing around. Good steps take real effort.
- In heavily featured snow, kick your foot into narrow ridges to knock away enough snow for a platform or merely step on a natural foothold.
- In less featured snow, aim your foot toward an existing depression because the snow is at a lower angle than the rest of the slope.
- Kick your foot as few times as possible per step, ideally only once. It is not unheard of to kick four times or more, but this will decrease speed and increase fatigue.
- Continually assess the snow and attempt to predict its hardness. Reflect on how easy or difficult it was to kick your steps in relation to what the snow looked like. By surveying the snow you can make microroutefinding decisions so that you kick your foot in the best possible location. The firmness of the snow can vary dramatically with each step, especially if the snow is in the sun. Move to the side

and try a new direction if the snow is too soft or too hard.

In softer snow, your foot may slip down or compress the snow below your foot as you make a step. This can scare people not used to kicking steps. After a while you will recognize the difference between the snow safely settling and being on the verge of falling.

When traveling in a group over difficult terrain, have the strongest members near the front so that they share the job of creating steps large enough for members at the rear. Be sure that the distance between steps is comfortable for all members of the party.

Every person in a group should kick his or her foot to improve the step. Kicking your foot, even if it is to only scrape away at where your sole will go, improves your grip. Steps can become slick and tilted downhill very quickly. You know you are doing it right when you are kicking snow into the legs of the person in front of you.

### Walking Technique or
### Pied Marché
The walking technique involves using the traction of the sole of your boot to grip the snow, just like walking down the street. The success of this technique is determined in part by the angle of the slope, the amount of traction on your boot, and the conditions of the snow. Basically this technique involves simply walking on snow or kicking your boot's sole against the snow so that your tread grips better.

Unless the slope is low angle and the snow is just the right hardness, rarely rely on this technique for gaining elevation. But if the conditions are just right, you can move quickly because you avoid expending extra energy kicking steps.

A very common error is to try to ascend steep snow (or snow-covered grass) the same way you would walk up a staircase. Merely setting your foot on the snow with the expectation that your boots' tread will grip is likely to fail. Once you start slipping, it is time to start kicking steps.

### Sidestepping or Zigzagging
Sidestepping means kicking the outside edge of one boot (pinky toe side) and the inside edge (big toe side) of the other into the snow. Swing from your knee, keeping the sole of your boot level or tilted slightly into the slope (Figure 2-2). Swing forward and slightly into the slope to make the biggest step you can (or need). (On very firm snow, swing your foot more into the slope than forward, sort of like front-pointing.) This motion is very different than merely stomping your foot into the snow in the hopes of compressing it to make a platform.

Your foot is angled slightly into the slope to create a stable platform. If the sole of your foot is angled slightly downslope, even if you kick a large platform your foot may slide off because that is the direction gravity is pulling it. Become proficient going left as well as right.

When using a sidestepping technique while heading diagonally, put one foot in front of the other. To sidestep straight up the slope, maintain an out-of-balance

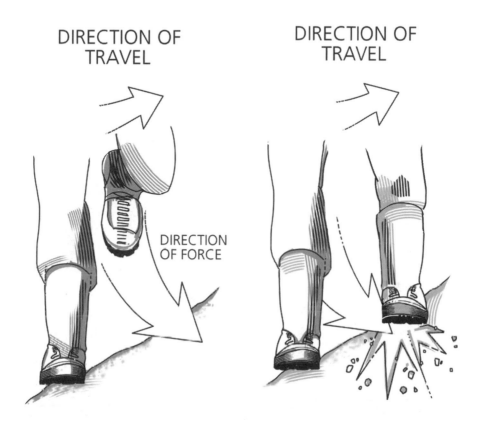

DIRECTION OF
TRAVEL

DIRECTION OF
TRAVEL

DIRECTION
OF FORCE

*Figure 2-2. Sidestepping is used to make a good step with the edge of your foot: your foot follows a curved path: swinging forward and into the slope.*

position (your downhill leg will remain in front and your uphill leg will stay behind you) as you almost "rock back and forth" between feet. A steeper line means taking a shorter route; this may be more energy efficient because you kick fewer steps, but each step may be more tiring because your steps gain more altitude than a low-angle zigzag would. Longer zigzags may be more tiring because you must kick more steps to gain the same elevation as you would going nearly straight up.

## WALKING IN-BALANCE

Walking in-balance is how you position your feet on a slope to remain comfortable and expend less energy when resting. When traversing or climbing diagonally up a slope, you always have what is referred to as an uphill and a downhill leg. Standing in-balance means you put almost all your weight on your downhill leg because it is straight, while your uphill leg is forward and bent (Photo 2-2).

On lower-angle slopes it is difficult to feel the benefits of standing in-balance versus standing out-of-balance (Photo 2-3). As the slope angle steepens beyond roughly 45 degrees, ending a set of steps in-balance is important for efficiently resting.

Photo 2-2. Standing in-balance

Photo 2-3. Standing out-of-balance

Photo 2-4. Before she turns right, the climber securely kicks her left foot into the snow and plants her ax.

Photo 2-5. Next, she kicks her right foot into the snow with her toe pointing in her new direction of travel and puts her left hand on top of the ax for stability.

Photo 2-6. She rotates the head of her ax so that her new uphill hand is holding the ax. She then steps through with her left foot and continues on.

## Pros

- Using the edge of your boot puts the maximum surface area of your boot against the snow, so this technique may provide the best security.
- Zigzagging up the slope may save energy because you gain less elevation with each step.
- Zigzagging works both sides of the foot and both arms which helps prevent fatigue on one side of your foot and body.

## Cons

- Long zigzags up a slope may take you underneath hazards higher on the mountain or over hazards below you.
- Long zigzags are time-consuming.

Changing directions while zigzagging efficiently saves time and reduces the risk of falling while switching the ax from one hand to another. Change directions safely by following these four steps, while holding the ax in the cane position or the self-arrest grip position. See Photos 2-4, 2-5, and 2-6.

1. Kick your downhill (left) foot securely into the snow; your ax should be in your uphill hand and planted directly uphill from you.
2. Kick your uphill (right) foot into the snow so that the "big toe" edge is securely planted. During this step both of your hands rest on the head of the ax.
3. Once you feel stable, rotate the shaft of your ax (while still keeping the spike in the snow), and slide your new uphill hand to the cane or self-arrest grip position on the ax.
4. Step through with your new uphill foot and continue climbing in the new direction. Move your ax first only if necessary.

### The Duck Step, *Pied en Canard*

Kicking steps with the duck step means heading up the fall line and kicking with the big toe side of each boot. Depending upon the flexibility of your hip, this technique works best when your feet straddle a ridge of snow or some convex feature (Photo 2-7).

Kick your foot in the same manner as you do for sidestepping. The only difference is you use the big toe side of each foot. The duck step does not always require the inside edge of your foot to rest entirely on the slope; it may be that only the inside edge of the ball of your foot rests on the snow. The greater the surface area of your boots on the snow, the more stable your steps will be.

*Photo 2-7. Using the duck step is easiest when you straddle a convex feature.*

**Pros**

■ It allows you to make as much upward progress per step as front-pointing, but provides the extra security of more surface area of your boots on the snow.

**Cons**

■ It is very difficult if you are inflexible and if the slope is featureless or concave.

### Front-Pointing, the German Technique

Traditionally the term front-pointing referred to using crampons and kicking the front points of crampons into the snow. Today it refers to kicking your toe straight in with or without crampons. When front-pointing, travel directly up the fall line or angle slightly. To front-point, kick the toe of your boot into the snow, keeping the sole of your boot horizontal or with the toe pointed slightly down so you make a small platform for your foot to rest on. Keeping your heel low is more energy efficient than keeping it high. Create the platform by compressing the snow in front of your foot or by knocking the snow to the side. The softer your boots and the firmer the snow, the more difficult this technique will be. Softer boots also require you to have your heels

higher because when your toe area flexes it will rotate and potentially angle your step down the slope.

When the snow is right and you feel strong, front-pointing is the fastest way up. The challenge of front-pointing in hard snow is that it becomes very difficult to compress the snow in front of your foot to create a platform or cavity. Look for a small protrusion of snow; by kicking into the upper portion of this, the snow you hit is knocked to the left and right, allowing you to create a platform for your foot instead of a cavity. In addition, modify your technique slightly by kicking your foot at an angle slightly less than perpendicular to

*Photo 2-8. The more rigid the sole of your boots, the easier front-pointing becomes.*

the snow (a slight duck step), effectively kicking away some of the snow to make a platform. Alternately, when these techniques fail or your calves are tired, sidestep so that more of your foot can rest on a platform and help you feel secure. A proficient climber in rigid boots may make a platform only a centimeter deep; in softer boots it is preferable to have a platform big enough for the ball of your foot to rest on the snow.

### Pros

■ You gain maximum elevation per step.
■ You take the shortest line toward an objective directly above you.
■ Facing directly into the slope allows you to lean your arms against your ax. This transfers some weight to your arms, taking weight off your legs.

### Cons

■ It is more tiring on your calves.
■ It offers less security because so little of your sole rests on the snow.
■ Facing into the slope reduces some of your visibility above and around you if you are bent over.

### Combination Technique, The American Technique, or *Pied Troisième*

The combination technique is simply front-pointing with one foot and kicking the inside edge against the snow with the other foot (Photo 2-9). This technique works best when you are going straight up. (The French term comes from the ballet stance, but it is commonly translated to mean that your feet are in the position of a

*Photo 2-9. When using the combination technique, front-point with one foot while using a sidestepping technique with the other.*

clock's hands at three o'clock.) Save energy by alternating your feet between a three o'clock and a nine o'clock position.

### Pros

■ You gain maximum elevation per step.
■ You take the shortest line toward an objective directly above you.
■ Because the angle created between your two feet is approximately 90 degrees, this technique is easier than the duck step for people with a less flexible pelvis.

### Cons

■ It is tiring on your calves.

■ Though more secure than a pure front-pointing technique, you must still rely on front-pointing for half your steps.

### Stomping Steps

The previous techniques for kicking steps are built around the concept of swinging your foot into the slope in order to chop out a platform. In some situations where the snow is soft at the surface and firm enough to support your weight deeper down, you might have an easier time climbing if you stomp the sole of your foot into the snow. This does sound a little bit like postholing, but your foot does not plunge as deep into the snow.

Stomping may be used more often in a maritime (wetter) snowpack, but this type of snow can exist on any mountain. Of course, you may encounter snow that requires a combination of stomping and kicking. Most of the altitude you gain will be the result of kicking steps.

### The Crust Buster

You may encounter snow with a breakable crust on top and deep, unconsolidated snow below. Before you resign yourself to postholing or a major route change, give this technique a try.

Essentially you are on your hands and knees with one hand on your ice ax and the other hand resting on the snow. The goal is to disperse your weight to avoid breaking the crust. Front-point with your feet just enough to break the crust. What gives your foot a platform to support you is pushing your foot against the crust, parallel to the slope angle, not down into the snow. (See Figure 2-3).

Unless the conditions are just right (or that bad!), I rarely use this technique. But when I have to use it, I make much faster

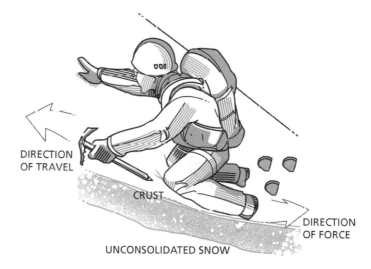

*Figure 2-3. To climb an area with a weak crust on top of unconsolidated snow, gently kick your foot through the crust and push parallel to the slope angle.*

DIRECTION OF TRAVEL

CRUST

DIRECTION OF FORCE

UNCONSOLIDATED SNOW

progress than other people who settle for postholing. This technique is best used to cross short sections of snow. If these conditions exist on a steep slope and over a large area, the avalanche hazard may be high.

### Pros

■ It helps you avoid postholing.

### Cons

■ Your knees may get cold and sore.

## CRAMPONS: TECHNIQUES FOR ASCENDING

In certain snow conditions, crampons are incredible. The feeling of stomping your foot into firm snow should bring about a sense of security. Wear crampons when the snow is either challenging or impossible to kick steps in, and when on ice. When used correctly on firm snow, the wedged spikes will penetrate deep into the snow and give you incredible traction, allowing you to walk on slopes that might otherwise make you nervous. Alternately, because you can travel on challenging terrain easily, you can get yourself into situations where falling may have serious consequences.

Bear in mind: Crampons are dangerous. Catching the spikes on your pants, gaiters, or boots may cause you to fall. Furthermore, if you do fall while wearing crampons, catching your spikes in the snow while you slide can generate enough force to break your leg. To avoid catching your crampons on your boots or clothing, heed the following tips: Keep boot laces short so that no loops exist after you tie them, or have long enough laces that you can tuck the loops behind the straps of your crampons; secure your gaiters over your pants to eliminate baggy material flapping around. Anything loose near your feet can pose a significant hazard when wearing crampons.

Another hazard of wearing crampons occurs when snow balls up under your feet and prevents the spikes from gripping the snow. Anti-balling plates (see Photo 1-4) can help reduce snow buildup. The best technique for cleaning your boots without slowing down is to hit the side of your boots (inside or outside edge) with your ax to knock off the snow. Staying balanced while doing this is easier if you keep moving instead of coming to a complete stop. Use your ax, not your ski pole; repeatedly hitting your boots or crampons with your ski pole will break it.

It can be a challenge to decide whether the risks of wearing crampons outweigh the benefits. Snow texture changes frequently over time and distance. If you take your crampons off as soon as you encounter packable snow, you might still encounter a patch of ice just below the surface. On the other hand, leaving your crampons on for too long after moving into packable snow may cause you to fall due to snow balling up under your crampons. Expect to put on and remove your crampons multiple times during a big climb.

It is important to become proficient at putting on and removing crampons so that time is not a factor in your decision to wear them or not. It is better to put crampons on early at a mellow resting spot rather than waiting until you slip on a steep slope.

Become proficient at putting crampons on with the points sticking in the snow and while your foot is in the air. This technique is important if you are standing in powdery snow. Make sure your crampons are on the correct foot (this means the buckle is on the outside of your foot) and your straps are tucked out of the way. Cut your straps so no more than 6 inches extends past the buckles after tightening them.

When you need to stow your crampons, fold the bindings flat, put them together with the points facing each other and the front points of one lined up with the heel points of another, and wrap the straps around the bundle to keep them together. To keep your points from tearing other items in your pack, either attach them to the outside of your pack or wrap them in a fleece jacket or stuff sack before stowing them in your pack.

Before venturing into the high peaks where tripping over your feet can have serious consequences, practice in a safe area. For difficult skills and steeper slopes, set up a top rope. Practice moving efficiently and confidently. The techniques used while wearing crampons are similar to those for kicking steps. The important difference when wearing crampons is that the spikes can trip you up.

You may have seen the bumper sticker, "Cowboy Up," which seems to be the cowboy equivalent of Nike's "Just Do It." Embrace a cowboy up, but also a "cowboy down," approach to your climbing. This means walking slightly bowlegged, with your toes pointing slightly outward (a slight duck step) to avoid catching your crampon points on the opposite leg.

### Walking Technique or *Pied Marché*
When you are wearing boots your ability to use the walking technique is limited by friction; when you are wearing crampons, the limits of this technique are defined by the flexibility of your ankle. However, even with flexible ankles this technique is confined to low-angle slopes.

The following techniques fit into three categories: flat-footed techniques, front-pointing, and the combination technique. When climbing, you will never rely on just a single technique. As the angle and firmness of the surface changes, so should the ways you use your feet. Use the technique that requires the least energy; this will usually mean having your foot flat against the slope until the slope angle requires front-pointing.

### The French Technique, *Pied à plat*
The French technique is a broad term for climbing with crampons and setting (or stomping) your foot into the snow so your downward facing points stick in it. To accomplish this you must let your ankles roll to the side. This flat-footed style is very similar to how you would "smear" your feet when walking across an angled slab of rock. The French technique becomes more difficult on steeper slopes and ice. As with all the techniques mentioned, look for irregularities in the snow surface that produce lower-angle areas for stepping onto.

## COMMON MISTAKES THAT LEAD TO INJURIES WHILE CLIMBING SNOW

*Accidents in North American Mountaineering* (American Alpine Club) is a publication that highlights some of the reported accidents that occur each year. Incidents have a description and possibly an analysis section where experts provide additional viewpoints. Anyone (professionals to beginners) who spends time in the outdoors would benefit from reading this publication. The following list has been generated from consulting this publication and other experts. Consider the following examples as a checklist of things to avoid doing.

- Intentionally and accidentally sliding on snow or ice while wearing crampons.
- Going too fast (for the conditions) while glissading down a slope. Examples of this include accelerating to a point where you lose control; going so fast that you are unable to stop before you encounter a hazard; and failing to notice the angle of the slope or firmness of the snow increasing, which then makes self-arresting impossible.
- Using ski poles instead of an ice ax in terrain where a fall is possible and the consequences of failing to self-arrest are high.
- Overestimating the ability of your pick or spike to support your weight if you fall. For the shaft or the pick to be used for support, more than just a point of balance, both must be driven most, if not all the way into firm snow. The easier it goes in, the easier it is going to pull out.
- Failing to adjust your climbing strategy with the changing of the seasons. For example, a slope you climbed in spring may have had a safe runout, but later in the summer, the snow has melted and exposed a boulder field at the base.
- Making a poor decision because you are tired. This may be failing to adjust your technique or leaving your crampons on when you should take them off.
- Overestimating your ability to self-arrest on steeper snow or ice.
- Attempting to move over snow in the same manner as another person instead of evaluating the terrain and making a decision based on your skill level.
- Traveling in a rope team with inexperienced climbers where if one member falls, they may pull the entire group down the slope.
- Not wearing a helmet in mountainous terrain. In addition to protecting your head from falling snow and rock, your helmet could keep you from slicing your forehead open with your adze.

The French technique is an invaluable tool for those who want to climb big mountains, but it's one that's missing from many climbers' toolboxes. Climbers with easy access to steep waterfalls may become proficient at climbing vertical ice and the intermediate slopes on the approach using the front-point method, but run into problems during long peak climbs. Front-pointing 3000 feet up a 40-degree slope has its problems. First, your calf muscles get exhausted, as will the auxiliary muscles you use while trying to balance on your toes for such a long time. Second, being forced to face the mountain will reduce your ability to continually observe your surroundings. Feeling comfortable walking in different ways gives you flexibility when the climbing gets "weird." Using one of the flat-footed techniques on very firm snow slopes between 10 and 50 degrees is an efficient way to climb.

**Sidestepping or Zigzagging:** The French technique is most commonly used for ascending a slope following a zigzagging path. You want to maintain a flat-footed technique so that all of your points stick in the snow (Photo 2-10). As with the side-stepping technique, you can follow a long, gradual ascent or ascend nearly parallel to the fall line. An advantage to following a zigzagging path (instead of front-pointing or using the duck step) is that it allows you to see more than just the slope above you and to your side; you also see what is behind you.

**The Duck Step**, *Pied en canard:* The duck step is merely a variation on the

*Photo 2-10. The French technique means walking up a slope while keeping the soles of your feet against the slope.*

French technique. The technique for the duck step while wearing crampons is the same as described in the kicking steps section, but you want to keep the soles of your feet against the snow. As the slope angle steepens, straddling a ridge with your feet makes this technique easier.

**Pros**

■ A flat-footed technique uses less energy than front-pointing.

**Cons**

■ As the slope angle steepens, supporting your weight with a flexed ankle becomes difficult.

■ It is difficult in stiff boots with limited ankle flex.

On steep slopes with firm snow and ice, staying flat-footed becomes dangerous because even if your points penetrate, gravity is trying to pull your foot down the slope. In soft snow a strict French technique is unnecessary and also potentially impossible since your points can no longer grip. Rather, kick your foot into the snow (keeping your boot horizontal) exactly as you did without crampons. Sometimes even after you step your foot into the snow you will find it more comfortable and stable to allow your ankle to flex so that all of your crampon points are in contact with the snow. On very hard snow and ice, keeping your feet flat against the surface is essential. Trying to edge on this brittle medium by keeping your foot horizontal (and using only the spikes on the uphill side of your crampon) is dangerous. Any torqueing motion by your foot may "pop" the ice around the spikes, causing you to lose your foothold. A technique created by Jeff Lowe addresses the danger of edging on brittle ice: Hedging, as Lowe calls it, involves stomping the uphill row of points of your crampons in the ice while the downhill row rests on the ice. This more stable platform keeps your foot from torqueing.

## The Combination Technique, the American Technique, *Pied Troisième* (The Three O'Clock Position)

As the slope angle increases, a flat-footed technique becomes difficult. The combination technique involves front-pointing with one foot and using the French technique with your other foot (Photo 2-11). This technique is a compromise between security and energy expenditure. Kicking your front points with one foot gives you security; flat footing (or edging) with the other saves energy. This technique works best for going straight up.

*Photo 2-11. The combination technique*

Photo 2-12. When flat-footing in stiff boots, it can be difficult to flex the ankle; use a four o'clock configuration.

Photo 2-13. Front-pointing

Save energy by alternating your feet between a three o'clock and a nine o'clock position.

Using this technique with very stiff leather boots or plastic mountaineering boots will require you to place your feet at a four o'clock and eight o'clock configuration (Photo 2-12).

### Pros

- You gain maximum elevation per step.
- You take the shortest line toward an objective above you.
- Because the angle created between your two feet is approximately 90 degrees, this technique is easier for people with a less flexible pelvis than a duck step on a smooth slope.

### Cons

- It is more tiring on your calves.
- On steep, very firm snow, the foot you edge with may feel insecure.

### Front-Pointing, the German Technique

Initially crampons had points that faced only down. This style required the climber to be proficient with a flat-footed technique. When front points were added in the 1920s, climbing changed dramatically. Climbers could ascend steep ice by front-pointing and rely even less on the ax. To front-point, kick the toe of your boot into the snow so the forward facing points of the crampons penetrate the surface (Photo 2-13). Keep the boot sole horizontal by lowering your ankles; this relaxed posture uses less energy and is more secure than having your heels elevated because you engage additional points of your crampons.

### Pros

■ You gain maximum elevation per step.
■ You take the shortest line toward an objective above you.
■ Facing directly into the slope allows you to lean your arms against your ax. This transfers weight to your arms, which takes weight off your legs.

### Cons

■ It is more tiring on your calves.
■ Facing the slope allows you to see what is ahead of you, but it becomes more difficult to look behind you.

### Additional Tips for Wearing Crampons

Although walking with crampons on rock will dull the points, sometimes it is not time efficient to take them off, for example, when moving along a boulder field between snow patches. Walking and scrambling on rocky terrain with crampons does require practice. Try to use either your front points, all of your points (step on a flat surface), or none of your points (step on fins of rock that are either parallel or perpendicular to your boot). If you try to step on rock using

only one side of your boot, you are at risk of twisting an ankle.

Postholing through unconsolidated snow above talus or boulders while wearing crampons is also a recipe for injury. Take off your crampons to dramatically reduce your chances of tripping or twisting a joint.

## TRANSITION ZONES

Transition zones are places where the terrain or snow changes significantly. Accidents are common in transition zones because they sometimes catch climbers off guard. Dramatic transitions occur between snow, ice, and rock, but they can also be subtle, e.g., between firm snow and powder. Terrain transitions include moving from a low-angled to a steep-angled slope, from an area with a safe runout to an area with a dangerous one, and from a protected, leeward side of a ridge to the cold, windward side.

Accidents happen because the medium or terrain can become suddenly difficult, and because climbers sometimes fail to adjust their equipment or technique in time. Always be alert in the mountains, looking ahead and paying attention with your senses, trying to detect changes in the snowpack and terrain well before you find yourself in dangerous zones.

For example, imagine walking along a trail that has an apron of snow covering one section. You see other hikers ahead who have successfully navigated the obstacle by kicking steps. You attempt to cross it by kicking steps as well, but halfway across you realize that you need your ice ax, which is strapped on your backpack. You may even have realized earlier that an ax would be useful, but you chose to keep going because it appeared from a distance that slipping would have minimal consequences. However, now you see that the snow extends beyond the trail and down the side of the mountain; slipping here would result in a very long fall. You must now choose between three less than desirable solutions: lose time by retracing your steps to safely get your ax, take your pack off to retrieve your ax in the middle of the steep slope, or proceed and risk a long fall. These risky options could have been avoided by grabbing your ax while standing on the trail.

Recognizing transitions before you get there will keep you safe and save you time. Keep essential equipment (e.g., ax, helmet, crampons, gloves, jacket) easily accessible. You may get some funny looks from hikers who stroll past while you are donning your helmet and crampons on easy terrain, but their facial expressions will change when you pass them later as they are crawling nervously across steeper ground without the right equipment.

## ENERGY CONSERVATION AND ROUTEFINDING SKILLS

When climbing rock, climbers continually look for places to put their hands and feet; climbing snow or ice should be no different. When the conditions are right, you can climb snow and ice as fast as your heart rate will allow because you can focus your eyes on the route without thinking too much about where to place your ax or feet. But even when ideal conditions do not exist, there are ways to reduce the workload on your brain and muscles.

- Start your climb long before the sun rises, especially if you are climbing on the south or east face of a peak.
- Look for natural depressions, no matter how small, to kick your steps into. Your goal is to get as much of the surface area of your boot's sole on the snow as possible. The closer to flat the snow is before you kick, the less energy will be needed to make a good step. This becomes more important the steeper the slope and the firmer the snow.
- Look for rocks that have fallen onto the snow and melted into the snow to provide a solid step. These can be especially important when the snow is very hard or soft because gaining ground requires only stepping onto the rock rather than having to kick.
- To avoid wasting time continually assessing your route over short distances, give yourself a distant point to aim toward that allows you to maintain a certain angle while ascending the slope. This point may be an obvious rock or feature on the snow. Use this landmark to mark where you plan to change directions or take a rest.

*Belay / run run Belay.*

- Choose the right level of protection for the snow conditions and the consequences of falling.
- Choose your resting locations wisely. Look ahead to find that natural depression or rock outcrop that allows you to really rest your muscles.
- Set the fastest pace you can without tiring or overheating. To help with this, use what's called the rest step (see Chapter 6), which involves taking a short break, one breath or a couple breaths long, while putting your weight on your skeleton so your leg muscles can rest.
- Keep track of hazards below and above you. Choose a route that reduces the consequences of falling and keeps you from traveling under hazards overhead.
- When climbing snow as a group, using each other's footsteps saves energy and can make the group faster if members alternate taking the lead. To switch out of the lead role, step to the uphill side of the group and kick your feet in so you are stable while other members travel below you.
- To avoid one climber slipping and hitting another, avoid climbing below other people when the climbing is difficult. A zigzagging path helps with this. Members should bunch up at the corners before the leader starts off in a new direction.
- When leading and following pitches during a roped ascent, climb faster when it is your turn because you will have a long rest when your partner is climbing. Beware of overheating and sweating too much.
- Be careful of ice lenses between the layers of snow and thin ridges of ice on the surface that run down the fall line. It is best to step over these or kick extra aggressive steps to break through them.

# Chapter 3

*Looking out toward the ocean from the slopes of Mount Alice in Alaska's Chugach Mountains*

# Using Your Ice Ax

*"Safety depends on unhurried speed."*
*—Gaston Rébuffat*

The ice ax has changed dramatically over time. Original models were designed more for walking than for technical travel and climbers also carried a shorter ax that could be used to chop steps. Later models combined the walking stick and ax features into a single tool. Before crampons made it easier to travel on steep snow, chopping steps was the main use for an ax. To facilitate step-chopping, the pick was straight and smooth which prevented it from getting stuck in the snow and ice. Now that crampons have dramatically reduced a climber's need to chop steps, the adze on the modern ice ax is designed for chopping while the pick is curved and has teeth that help it to stick the snow and that can be used for hooking.

## CARRYING YOUR ICE AX

Carry your ax using one of these four options (for storing it out of the way):
- The most out-of-the-way place to attach your ax is the ice ax strap on your backpack. Some packs have very loose or poorly configured straps that may cause the pick of your ax to stick out and be a hazard to others. If this is the case, after sliding the ax through the loop on your pack (Photo 3-1), hold the shaft horizontal, and spin the shaft so that the loop tightens around the head before you tilt your ax against your pack as shown in Photo 3-2. Make sure that when you tilt your ax up against your pack, the strap goes under the head preventing your ax from sliding out. Spinning the shaft in

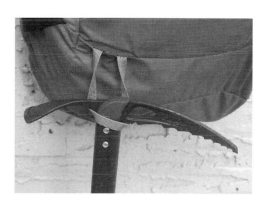

*Photos 3-1 and 3-2. To correctly attach your ax to your pack, first slide the shaft with the pick facing toward the middle of the pack down through the ice ax loop. Next, tilt the ax upward so that the loop wraps around the head (preventing your ax from sliding downward) and secure the shaft to your pack.*

*Photo 3-3. Three ways to carry your ice ax when you are not using it for climbing, but want it accessible*

the correct direction is essential because the tension created by twisting the strap helps push the pick against the pack. In Photo 3-1, the shaft would be spun clockwise if the strap were loose.

■ Once your ax is out, the most convenient way to store it is to slide the shaft between the shoulder straps of your pack and your back (See Photo 3-3). Safely stored, from this location the ax can also easily be taken out without removing your pack. Be careful taking your pack off, however; since your ax is not actually attached to anything, it can fall out. When not wearing a pack you can slide the shaft between outer layers of your clothing. This method is not ideal but can work in a pinch.

■ When walking with an ax while on trails or other benign terrain, holding the ax by the shaft with the spike forward helps you keep better track of the pointed end of the ax, thus avoiding jabbing someone behind you with the spike (Photo 3-3). Hold the ax with the pick facing downward. Alternately, hold the ax by the head with the spike hanging by your side.

■ A short ax may be attached to the side of a pack, with the pick facing backward, using the compression straps. Retrieving your ax from this location by yourself is difficult.

When you are wearing a climbing harness, sliding your ax into one of the gear loops makes for convenient storage. However, having the ax at your side may be awkward if you are scrambling.

Train yourself to avoid dropping your ax. Even if you plan on using a leash, you should not have your hand through a leash most of the time. To avoid losing your ax follow these guidelines:

■ Hold the ax correctly for the medium in which you are traveling. If you are holding it incorrectly, you may fumble with it trying to readjust it in your hands.

*Photo 3-4. Stepping over a void while traveling downhill: Note the head of the ice ax should be in your downhill hand.*

- Never set your ax down on snow or ice; instead, swing the pick or jab the spike far enough in to keep it from falling.
- If you are on rocky terrain and need to set your ax down, laying it down is typically better than leaning it against something. Lay it out of the way of other climbers.

For all but a handful of situations, having the ax in your uphill hand makes going up, traversing, and going down safer and easier. Make this a habit! If heading straight up with both hands at equal height, alternate hands so you become proficient with both.

There are some situations that would cause a climber to break this golden rule:

- **Jumping or stepping over a void** while descending a low-angle slope (Photo 3-4). In this situation keep your ax in your uphill hand until just before making the crossing. It's better to have your ax in your downhill hand in this situation because if you land poorly, you can

*Photo 3-5. Investigating a hazard above you: Hold your ax with the head in your downhill hand so you can fall into the self-arrest position more easily if you slip.*

fall into the self-arrest position (see Chapter 5) and avoid falling into the crevasse, creek, or moat between the rock and snow. Holding your ax in one hand allows you to jump further than having your ax in both hands.

■ **When you must investigate a hazard** (e.g., a void or ridge) to your uphill side (Photo 3-5). Your concern in this situation is having to fall into the self-arrest position if the lip breaks, with solid ground to your downhill side. Hold the ax in the self-arrest position to reduce your chances of falling into or off something.

■ **Walking along the spine of a ridge** may be much easier and faster than trying to traverse along one of the sides. Because the ground drops away to both sides, technically, there is no uphill side. It is likely that one of the sides would be much worse to fall down than the other. If the side you do not want to fall off is to your left, hold the head of your ax in your right hand.

An ice ax has four main uses: providing a point of balance while you climb, acting as an artificial hold to help support you as you climb, helping you stop if you fall, and chopping steps or platforms into the snow or ice.

There is no hierarchy for the following eight ice ax techniques; each has advantages and disadvantages in any given situation. Choose the technique based on the level of security you need, the amount of energy required to use the technique, and the amount of time it takes to plant your ax. Never just set your ice ax on the snow or ice when taking a break. Always either swing the pick or jab the spike deep into the snow to keep it from sliding away.

Becoming proficient at climbing snow requires feeling comfortable performing all of the following techniques with either hand. Spend time practicing with your less dominant hand if necessary.

## USING THE SPIKE AS A POINT OF BALANCE OR SUPPORT

Using the spike of your ax (versus the pick) as a point of balance or support allows you to maintain an upright position with your body and keep your weight over your feet. On firm snow and ice, having a sharp spike is essential.

### PIOLET CANNE

The standard technique for holding your ax while you ascend, *piolet canne* translates to holding the ice ax like a cane (Photo 3-6). As you climb, grip the head of the ax while resting the heel of your hand on the adze, and jab the spike into the snow just enough to give you a point of balance. Use your ice ax to help you balance; you are not jabbing it in deep enough to act as a support you can pull on to keep from falling. Your security should come from your feet. Use this technique when falling is of little concern.

**Pros**

■ This grip is more comfortable for your hand than the self-arrest grip.

■ It is easy to transition from it to the other daggering techniques.

*Photo 3-6. Holding the ax in* piolet canne *with the spike in the snow*

*Photo 3-7. Holding the ax with the self-arrest grip with the spike in the snow*

- Your hand on the adze with the pick facing forward makes you less susceptible to impaling yourself with the pick.

**Cons**

- Self-arresting is more difficult than with the self-arrest grip (because you must switch to the self-arrest grip before you can jab the pick into the snow).
- It gives you less reach and a less secure hold on the ax than a self-arrest grip does.

### SELF-ARREST GRIP

The self-arrest grip should be used when falling is a real possibility, when descending while facing sideways or facing out, when glissading, and during roped team travel on

a glacier when you may need to self-arrest to catch a team member who has fallen into a crevasse. As you climb, grip the head of your ax with your thumb and index finger under the adze, and jab the spike into the snow just enough to give you a point of balance (Photo 3-7). Keep the adze pointed forward. Your ax is for balance, not for jabbing it in deep enough to act as an anchor to keep you from falling.

If you are using your spike as your point of contact with the snow and you are concerned about falling, this technique puts you in a better position for arresting your fall than the cane grip because you will only need to grab the shaft with your other

## TECHNIQUES FOR YOUR AX
### (*PIOLET* IN FRENCH)

The following table lists the French and English terms for the most common ax techniques. It starts with the techniques used on flatter terrain and progresses to those you would use as the slope gets steeper.

| NAME: FRENCH | NAME: ENGLISH | |
|---|---|---|
| *Piolet canne* (pronounced: PEE-oh-lay cahn) | Cane grip | |
| Variation of *piolet canne* | Self-arrest grip | |
| N/A | Stake grip | |

*Table 3-1*

| NAME: FRENCH | NAME: ENGLISH | |
|---|---|---|
| N/A | Self belay | |
| *Piolet panne*<br>(pronounced:<br>PEE-oh-lay pahn) | Low dagger | |
| *Piolet poignard*<br>(pronounced:<br>PEE-o-lay pwoi-NEEAHR) | High dagger | |
| *Piolet manche*<br>(pronounced:<br>PEE-oh-lay mahn-SH) | N/A | |
| N/A | Self-arrest position | |

## TECHNIQUES FOR YOUR AX (CONTINUED)

| NAME: FRENCH | NAME: ENGLISH | |
| --- | --- | --- |
| N/A | Single overhead swing | |
| *Piolet traction*<br>(pronounced:<br>PEE-oh-lay trac-seeohn) | Dual overhead swing | |
| *Piolet ramasse*<br>(pronounced:<br>PEE-o-lay RAHM-ahss) | Cross-body position | |
| *Piolet rampe*<br>(pronounced:<br>PEE-oh-lay RAH-mp) | N/A | |

## SELF-ARREST GRIP VERSUS CANE GRIP

From a historical perspective the cane grip is the original technique; it is also what most Europeans and climbing guides use when there is a choice between the cane and self-arrest grips. On the other hand, many climbers use the self-arrest grip only. Make your decision based on your experience and situation. On steep, firm snow, using the cane grip may give you more balance, which prevents you from falling. The main purpose of your ice ax while walking on a lower-angle portion of a glacier is to catch someone else's fall into a crevasse; therefore, the self-arrest grip is the logical choice. Get out and practice both techniques while keeping in mind that "never" and "always" rarely apply to climbing.

hand and force the pick into the snow to self-arrest. This technique is most relevant on lower-angle slopes where an inexperienced climber may fall. On steep frozen snow (and ice), arresting a fall is almost impossible; therefore, choose a technique that will best keep you from falling.

**Pros**

- If you slip, your hand is in the proper position for self-arresting.
- It is easy to transition from it to the high dagger technique.

**Cons**

- It is a less comfortable position for the hand than the cane position.

### STAKE GRIP

This grip works well when you are climbing straight up a fall line. Hold the head with one hand on the adze and one hand over the pick. If falling and self-arresting is a possibility, hold the head of the ax in self-arrest grip with one hand, and place your other hand on the adze (Photo 3-8).

*Photo 3-8. The stake grip*

If the shaft penetrates more than half its length into the snow, you are starting to use a variation on this technique called the self-belay (see below).

### Pros

- Using two hands increases the force for driving the spike deep into the snow.
- Having both hands on the head is more stable when resting.
- It allows you to move to the self-arrest position quickly.

### Cons

- Having both hands on the head of the ice ax while climbing prevents you from having one hand free to help with balance.
- Touching metal with both hands may lead to colder hands.

## SELF-BELAY TECHNIQUE

The self-belay technique entails using the self-arrest grip (one hand) or stake grip (two hands), but jabbing the shaft of the ax as deeply into the snow as possible to serve as a temporary anchor in the event of a fall (Photo 3-9). Use this technique if you can push the shaft in all (or most of) the way to the head. Push the ax in vertically or tip it no more than 30 degrees back from perpendicular in the upslope direction. This technique is practical only when the snow is soft enough to plunge the shaft into the snow, but firm enough that the ax has a chance of holding if pulled downhill. In the right kind of snow, this technique provides great security; it is most useful when used for occasional rests or when you need some added protection because there is a hazard a short distance below.

### Pros

- It provides a secure anchor.

Photo 3-9. For the self–belay, pushing the entire shaft into the snow allows your ax to act as a point of protection you can hold on to if you slip.

### Cons

- Driving the shaft deep into the snow every time you move your ax is time-consuming and tiring.

If you are relying on the self-belay to hold your weight in a fall, or as a clip-in point, grab the shaft with your free hand (Photo 3-10) or attach your webbing to the ax where it is sticking out of the snow, not to the head (unless the ax has been driven in all the way). The reason for this is that the farther the ax is sticking out of the snow, the more leverage the load will

*Photo 3-10. If your ax penetrates only partway into the snow and you slip, grab the shaft with your free hand to hold the head to reduce the chances of your ax leveraging out.*

*Photo 3-11. The tilting stake 1: Lean forward and plant the spike in snow.*

*Photo 3-12. The tilting stake 2: Leaving the spike where it is, continue to kick steps up the slope until your feet catch up to your ax.*

have, thus the easier the ax will tilt downward and pull out. The security of this placement will depend upon the firmness of the snow, how deep the ice ax goes in, and the direction of pull. Your direction of pull should always be down the slope. An accidental upward pull could occur if you are clipped into the ax with a short leash and you stand up. If the ax will not go in all the way, try hammering on the head with another ax, your foot, or a rock.

### THE TILTING STAKE

When the snow and slope angle combined provide secure travel without using your ax with every step or two, this technique will help you move faster and vary your climbing style. Instead of planting your ax nearly straight up and down, lean forward and point the spike into the snow while the shaft is nearly horizontal; this gives you a point of balance (Photo 3-11). As you climb leave the spike in its original position (Photo 3-12) and let the shaft rotate to a vertical position. Move the ax upward when your feet get close to it. This technique works best for intermediate angled slopes. On lower and steeper angled slopes you will either lean too far forward or too far back respectively.

#### Pros
- It reduces fatigue and lets you climb faster.

#### Cons
- It is less stable than moving your ax every other step, especially on steep slopes.
- It adds stress to upper body muscles.

## TECHNIQUES THAT DRIVE THE PICK INTO THE SNOW FOR BALANCE OR SUPPORT

As the angle steepens and the snow becomes firmer, planting the spike requires lifting your hand higher and pushing harder, thus using more energy. This is when your ax's pick takes over. The following five techniques use the ax as a point of support to keep a slip from becoming a fall. Stopping yourself should you fall is covered in the chapter on self-arresting; however, it is important to understand that falling while climbing steep, hard snow is not advised! The goal is to climb quickly and securely to avoid falling. Do not rely on these pick techniques when you should be standing and using your ax as a point of balance. Leaning your upper body against a low-angle slope can be quite tiring.

*Daggering* is a general term used to describe pushing the pick into the snow. Except in very hard snow, the pick must penetrate almost entirely to provide real support. Even then the snow must be firm enough to hold your weight. No equation exists for determining stability; you must learn through experience.

When daggering with only one hand on the ax, move your hands upward by alternating which hand is on the snow. You can either "walk" your hands up the slope by placing your ax-free hand or your hand with the ax higher up than where the other is positioned. Alternatively, shuffle your hands upward by moving the hand with the ax first and then bring the other hand to the same level, then repeat. Save time and energy by moving your hands as far upward as is comfortable and moving your feet as high as possible before moving your ax again.

### LOW DAGGER, *PIOLET PANNE*

Low dagger, or *piolet panne,* is used on moderate slopes to provide balance while you climb facing straight in (Photo 3-13). Position your hand on the head exactly as you would for the cane grip. As you ascend,

Photo 3-13. Using the low dagger while "walking" your hands up the slope and front-pointing is an efficient way to climb. The next move for this climber will be to take another step with his right foot and jab the pick into the snow higher up than his right hand.

push the pick into the snow at about chest level, and climb as high as possible before moving your ax again. The low dagger is an efficient technique and provides some security if you slip when your ax is below your elbow because you can push against it. For some additional support, you can combine the low dagger and self belay by pushing both the pick and spike into the snow.

Using this technique (and *piolet manche*) on low-angle slopes will put more weight on your arms and tire them out. One advantage to leaning forward is that you can move quickly through a short section by distributing the weight between your four appendages so your legs can propel you faster. When descending, you can reach below your waist and push the pick into the snow to give you support before moving your feet downward.

**Pros**

- ▣ It provides a third point of support to prevent a fall.
- ▣ It is more comfortable and less tiring than the high dagger because you can keep the ax lower and use your body weight to force the pick into the snow.
- ▣ Your glove stays drier because less of it touches the snow compared to the high dagger.

**Cons**

- ▣ Self-arresting is more difficult than it is with the high dagger.

### *PIOLET MANCHE*

The *piolet manche* is similar to the low dagger and is used for balance and support while facing into the slope (Photo 3-14).

*Photo 3-14. Using* piolet manche, *the climber shuffles his hands upward by placing his ax-free hand at the same height as his left hand. His next move will be to climb upward with his feet and dagger with his left hand higher up the slope.*

Grip the shaft just below the head and punch the pick into the snow. The *piolet manche* is most effective when used from waist level to above your head.

### Pros
- Having one hand free provides balance when you are moving the ax.

### Cons
- Your hand could slide off the ax if your feet slip.
- If the pick fails to penetrate, as it may in very firm snow, the entire shaft may rotate, leaving you without a hold.
- Fingers and gloves are more vulnerable to wet and cold.

## HIGH DAGGER, *PIOLET POIGNARD*

Use the high dagger, or *piolet poignard*, for support on the steepest slopes when facing in. Hold the ax with your thumb under the adze and fingers over the top of the head (Photo 3-15). Stab the pick into the snow higher than your shoulder. Rest the palm of your other hand against the snow to provide balance.

### Pros
- It makes self-arresting easier and quicker.
- In tight spaces, it is easier to get the pick in than it is with the overhead swing.
- It provides a solid point of protection in firm snow, and is easier to remove than using the single overhead swing.

### Cons
- Having your free hand on the snow increases the chances of your hand getting wet and cold.

## SELF-ARREST POSITION

Reserve this ax position for times when there is the greatest likelihood that your ax will need to provide support. Holding your ax with two hands gives you the best chance of holding on, but it decreases your freedom

Photo 3-15. The high dagger easily allows you to transition to a self-arrest position should you slip.

Photo 3-16. The self-arrest position. If you are having trouble staying balanced, place your knee against the slope to give yourself three points of contact before you move your ax again.

to move your arms independently. Hold the head of the ice ax just as you did for the high dagger, and grip the shaft down toward the spike. Jab the pick into the snow while holding the shaft diagonally (Photo 3-16).

Move your hands upward when you feel too scrunched. If you feel off balance when moving your hands, use your knee(s) for balance. This technique will feel awkward if the snow is too hard for you to get the pick deep enough into the snow. Use one of your knees against the snow to provide balance while you make multiple attempts to jab the pick into the snow. If your efforts are futile, use the overhead swing technique.

*Photo 3-17.* Piolet ramasse

**Pros**

■ It provides greater security because you have both hands on your ax.

**Cons**

■ Having both hands on the ax limits the ability for your arms to move independently.

### ADVANCED TECHNIQUE: *PIOLET RAMASSE*

*Piolet ramasse* is one of the "classic" skills developed in Europe in the era before front points. Hold the head of your ax in your downhill hand (using the cane grip) and hold the shaft near the spike with your uphill hand (Photo 3-17). Push the spike into the snow to provide balance. Holding the ax in this manner is meant to keep your weight over your feet by pushing your upper body into a more upright position. This technique is most commonly used with crampons because it encourages a flat-footed climbing style. It is not often used, but it is a good additional piece for your "toolbox" for firm snow and steeper angles. Use this technique to ascend at a diagonal angle or to traverse. Consider this technique as well when crossing steeper slopes with a ski pole or walking stick.

### Pros

■ It forces your weight over your feet, which can increase your balance.

### Cons

■ Holding the head of the ax in your downhill hand makes dropping into the self-arrest position awkward.

■ It is very awkward with a short ax.

## SWINGING TECHNIQUES

If you need the ax for support on very firm snow, you need more force than daggering provides. Swinging is superior to daggering in very firm snow and ice.

### SINGLE OVERHEAD SWING

This is your best technique for gaining a solid placement in hard snow and ice. Hold the ax with your hand at the bottom of the shaft. If you are using a leash, it should come tight on your wrist, thus reducing the load on your fingers. Swing the ax from your elbow, not your shoulder (Photo 3-18). This is where having an ax with a heavier steel head pays off, because you need to swing a lighter ax much harder than a heavy ax to make it stick deep. If the pick barely penetrates, reduce your chances of leveraging the ax out of the snow by keeping your elbow against the snow. To prevent fatigue, keep your arm straight whenever possible to hang on your bones rather than your muscles.

Your other hand can be used for balance or for swinging another ax if you have one. The single overhead swing is best used when ascending straight up the slope. Using this while zigzagging feels awkward, but it can be done; swing the ax from your downhill hand.

This technique can be combined with the self-arrest position to create an effective means of climbing a short, steep section with only one swing of your ax. See the "Climbing Over a Lip" section.

### COMBINING THE ICE AX WITH KICKING STEPS

On steep, firm snow, plant your ax in rhythm with your feet so that you maintain two points of contact with the snow at all times. When moving quickly, you can have one point of contact by moving your arm and one foot at the same time. A typical rhythm is as follows: step, step, plant your ax ahead of you. Move your ax when standing in-balance.

*Photo 3 18. The single overhead swing*

### Pros
- It allows strong force for driving the pick deep into the snow.
- The ax can act as a handhold to help you make upward progress or catch you if you slip.
- It allows you to reach high above your head to hook rocks, trees, etc.

### Cons
- Swinging your ax every few steps is time- and energy-consuming.
- Self-arresting may be difficult if your arm is fully extended when you fall.
- Removing the pick as you climb past it requires more energy.

## CUTTING OR CHOPPING STEPS AND PLATFORMS

Cutting steps is an essential skill that involves using your adze or pick to chip away at snow or ice to create a set of steps when the snow is too firm for kicking into. Cutting steps is one of the oldest snow climbing techniques and is useful for occasionally improving a step and for climbing

CUT

CUT CUT CUT CUT
1   2   3   4   5

DIRECTION OF TRAVEL

*Figure 3-1. Cut steps by swinging your ax in a methodical fashion to lengthen a step away from you. (The size of the steps has been exaggerated for clarity; cut steps only as large as needed.)*

### LEARNING FROM EXPERIENCE: CUTTING STEPS

A warm day followed by a calm, clear night is the perfect recipe for waking up to a mountainside of frozen summer snow. I discovered this firsthand during a backpacking trip with friends in Colorado some years ago. During some free time in camp, I kicked steps up the soft afternoon snow to see our route for the next day. Even a late start the next morning would not have affected the snow conditions because we were on the north side of a ridge tucked in between two peaks. When we reached our slope, we found it much too firm for kicking steps. My steps from the day before solved our dilemma. In a few places where my steps were inadequate we cut a few steps with our axes. Without the steps we would have had to wait until the snow softened in the afternoon. Conclusion: Even in summer, a solid freeze can occur. While kicking steps the day before is an option, cutting steps really pays off when you need it.

sections of snow too firm for kicking steps but not large enough to necessitate putting on crampons. It may also be worth cutting steps when climbing with an inexperienced partner who would benefit from bigger steps.

## HOW TO CUT STEPS

The basic idea of cutting steps involves swinging the adze against the snow to create a concave depression. The first swing should carve out the portion of the step closest to you. With each successive swing the adze chops away at the far end of your initial concave depression until the step is large enough to stand on (Figure 3-1). Cutting steps efficiently requires methodic technique. Haphazard swings will force you to spend more time chopping.

The following three examples illustrate chopping steps on progressively steeper slopes.

■ When climbing a slope with an angle too low for you to easily lean your hand against as a point of balance, start with the ax in your uphill hand. Walk upward in a sidestepping manner, cutting one or two steps at a time. When cutting steps in ice, angle the steps into the slope to prevent you from sliding off. Use your ax as a point of balance if you are feeling insecure trying to step up. A walking stick or trekking pole in your other hand may be useful as a point of balance.

■ When the slope angle increases so that you can comfortably place your uphill hand against the slope as a point of balance, hold the ax in your downhill hand

Photo 3-19. Chopping steps at a diagonal angle with the ax in the downhill hand. Whenever you chop steps, consider the consequences of sliding into whatever is below you because self-arresting is likely to be impossible.

(Photo 3-19). Swing the adze as described above and continue to cut only one or two steps ahead of your feet. If you feel comfortable without a hand on the slope, you may hold the ax in your uphill hand.

Photo 3-20. Chopping steps up a very steep slope

**LEARNING FROM EXPERIENCE:**
**THAT LAST 20 FEET AND A HEAVY BACKPACK**

A few years ago I went to Colorado's Elk Mountain Wilderness, which has some great snow climbing. It was early in the morning and I was on the shady side of the peak, where the snow was hard. From below, the steep headwall of the gully appeared to have an easy exit, but when I got there I realized I was wrong. Attempting to climb this steep section with a heavy backpack seemed like a bad idea, so I removed it and wedged it ever so slightly between the rock wall and the snow (I could also have chopped out a platform in the snow). I tied a 30-foot piece of cord securely to the backpack and loosely to my wrist. I finished the climb, hauled my pack up, and continued on my way.

As long as you can find a secure place to stash your pack, this technique may give you that extra bit of confidence for a small but difficult section. Four things should never happen while using this technique: you or your pack falling, underestimating the length of the climb relative to your amount of cord, wedging your pack so tightly that you are unable to retrieve it by pulling on the cord, and using cord that may fail under the load. Any of these scenarios may result in you, your pack, or both falling down the slope. Having the cord loosely draped over your wrist allows you to escape disaster if your pack falls because you accidentally pulled on the cord or you set it in a precarious position. If you are climbing with a partner, the second climber can hold the packs secure while the first person climbs over the edge. The leader can then haul the packs before the second climber climbs.

■ On really steep slopes where walking diagonally feels awkward, face into the slope. Stand still and cut steps from just above your feet to approximately waist height (Photo 3-20). Then move your feet upward with your toes facing in, but do not move higher until you have cut a new step or two at waist height. Cutting steps is easier if you move your hand partway up the shaft of your ax and use an up and down hammerlike motion to chop away at the snow. The benefit of moving straight uphill is that you can alternate hands for chopping steps.

While chopping steps may help you travel where kicking steps would be impossible, do not forget to consider the consequences of falling. Self-arresting on terrain where you need to cut steps is probably impossible. A route that requires you to chop steps for long distances is probably a route on which you should be wearing crampons.

Practice this technique before venturing out onto bulletproof snow or ice. Find a location where you can "boulder" or set up a top rope without worrying about the consequences of falling.

*Photo 3-21. Climbing up a slope using two axes with each hand in the low dagger position*

## CLIMBING WITH TWO AXES

For peak climbing, climbers usually bring one ax unless the climbing is particularly difficult; when it is difficult they are likely to bring ropes and protection as well. There are situations in which two axes make climbing more secure. The key is determining what each ax will be used for. What follows are some common ways of incorporating two axes into your climbing.

■ Both axes in the low dagger or *piolet manche.* Climb just as you would with only one ax in these positions (Photo 3-21).

■ Double overhead swing. Use two axes in this manner only on the most difficult slopes. Climbing with two axes like this takes more time than using one. North American mountaineers commonly refer to this as *piolet traction.*

■ Mixing the low dagger with the overhead swing combines the security of swinging your ax with the speed of daggering.

■ A strategy on lower-angle slopes is to walk with a ski pole in your downhill hand to provide balance and to help push you forward. Carry an ax in your uphill hand using the cane or self-arrest grip.

## CLIMBING OVER A LIP

The crux of many routes is climbing over a steep lip at the top. This final set of moves may be more risky because usually the slope angle at the top will be steeper and self-arresting more difficult. These are important skills to practice somewhere safe.

Climbing over the lip in soft snow is an art. One approach is to kick steps gently so they do not collapse. The other approach is to kick more aggressively, hoping that you will reach firm snow deeper in. If the snow is really soft, push the shaft of the ax into the snow in a slightly more than horizontal angle and then hold the shaft where it protrudes from the snow to prevent leveraging it out (Photo 3-22).

The technique *piolet ancre* (meaning "to anchor," pronounced *onkr*) combines the single overhead swing with the self-arrest position to create the following sequence of moves (See Photos 3-23—3-25).

In firm snow, climbing over a short (one to two body lengths) headwall using the minimum amount of movements looks like this: With your feet as high as you can comfortably put them, use the single overhead

*Photo 3-22. Plunging the shaft, instead of the pick, into the snow may work better for climbing over a lip in soft snow.*

*Photo 3-23, top left. When climbing over a steep lip, start with a solid overhead swing.*

*Photo 3-24, top right. Grabbing the head of the ax will give you a firm grip as you move your feet upward.*

*Photo 3-25 bottom left. From this position, continue moving your feet upward and repeat the sequence or use the self-belay technique to secure your ax for the final moves to climb over the lip.*

(Photos by Robert Buswold)

swing so that your pick sticks firmly in the snow. Begin kicking steps, most likely by front-pointing. When your feet are high enough, grab the ax head in the high dagger position with your other hand. Continue to kick steps and switch hands on the ax so the hand you swung with is now resting on the adze in a low dagger position. When your feet are at their highest (ideally your feet should be nearly as high as the head of your ax) and secure, remove your ax from the snow and repeat these steps as necessary. Try and make your final moves over the lip as graceful as possible by continuing to kick good steps because you do not want to rely entirely on your ax if you can help it.

Becoming proficient using an ice ax is one of those skills that opens a lot of doors for climbing and is essential for getting you out of trouble. It only adds a small amount of weight to your pack, but having an ax handy on a climb will give you the freedom to climb a snowy route if the trail is full of people or quickly descend a snow slope before the afternoon thunderstorm rolls in. Once you become proficient with each of these skills, your next step will be to progress beyond applying the right tool in the right situation, to switching from one technique to another in a fluid motion. When this happens, your climbing will become more graceful.

# Chapter 4

*Descending the lowest portion of Exit Glacier, Kenai Mountains of Alaska*

# Descending

*"You're not up 'til you're down."*

Mental and physical fatigue play a major role in accidents that occur during descents. Your first line of defense is to prepare for your descent before it begins. If Mother Nature allows it, take a break at your high point. Drink, eat, and dress for the conditions because you will generate less heat while descending. Have your headlamp on your helmet or in your jacket pocket, just in case darkness descends faster than you do. Mentally prepare for descending, and if you are tired, acknowledge it and follow steps (e.g., double checking each other) to avoid making mistakes.

Be safe and have fun. On popular climbs, especially at dusk or in bad weather, move efficiently to avoid getting caught at a "bottleneck" behind other groups.

The following techniques are listed starting with those you would use on more difficult terrain (steeper and firmer snow) and ending with those you would use on easier terrain (lower-angle slopes with softer snow).

## DESCENDING OVER AN EDGE

When descending from a summit or ridge onto the side of a mountain, the first few meters may be the steepest. Climbing down the edge is similar to climbing over it. If your route requires you to take this steep headwall down, look for the lowest angle, the shortest headwall, and the best snow. Consider your runout should you fall, but avoid taking a more dangerous route just because the runout is better.

Begin descending by planting your ice ax near enough to the edge to allow

*Photo 4-1. The first step in descending a lip is to get your feet onto the lower slope.*

*Photo 4-2. Descending diagonally by chopping steps* (Photo by Steve Langford)

you to maintain a good grip on the ax and also kick your feet into the slope below (Photo 4-1).

Move your feet as far down as possible before moving the ax again. If the snow near the top is firm, chop a few steps for your feet into the slope below before planting your ax. Following a slightly curved path over the edge will allow you to keep your arms straighter, thus using your muscles less.

Once your body is entirely below the edge and you have kicked secure steps for your feet, move your ax down from the edge and choose from the following techniques.

Descending over the edge may be easier with multiple tools or if steps already exist from your ascent. If traveling in a group, consider using your auxiliary cord as a means for shuttling axes to the top so that each climber has two tools.

## CHOPPING STEPS

Knowing how to use your adze to chop steps into hard snow or ice is essential because you may be able to avoid putting on crampons or turning back. However, depending on how far you have to chop steps and the runout below, it may be more efficient to put on crampons.

Chopping steps while descending is easiest when you follow a diagonal path. Hold a previous step with your uphill hand or place it against the slope for balance. Hold the ax in your downhill hand. Swing your ax so the adze cuts out a small wedge of snow. Your first swing should be closest

*Photo 4-3. Front-pointing and holding the ax in the self-arrest position is an efficient way to move down a steep section of snow.*

to you. Additional swings will be away from you, lengthening your step. Cut one step at a time; move your feet down one at a time. It is typically much more difficult to step down from your downhill leg (because you are crossing your legs) so make this step lose less elevation as shown in Photo 4-2. When stepping down from your uphill leg, cut your step as far down as you can comfortably step.

### Pros
- It is a secure method of descending without crampons.

### Cons
- Chopping steps is a slow process.
- Self-arresting will be unlikely if you fall.

## DOWNHILL STEP TECHNIQUES

### FRONT-POINTING
In his inspiring book *Climbing Ice,* Yvon Chouinard recommended not facing the slope during descent, except as a last resort because it is hard to see below you. When the snow is hard, the slope is steep, and the route is clear below you, however, front-pointing is a great technique. While considered a slow technique by many climbers, with some practice you can become efficient and fast (Photo 4-3).

Hold the ice ax in the self-arrest position and kick your toes into the snow (see "front-pointing" under the kicking steps

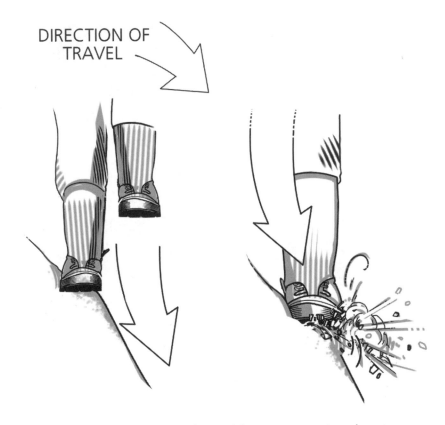

DIRECTION OF
TRAVEL

Figure 4-1. On firm snow, you can stomp your foot and shave away snow to make a step.

section). To move quickly, follow a "kick, kick, move the ax down" sequence where your feet move past each other. Increase security (but go slower) by taking smaller steps and letting your knees rest against the snow while you move your ax. Moving faster means you are less likely to tire your legs. To avoid accidentally kicking into an elephant trap (see Chapter 7 on Hazards) or over an edge, periodically look down and then travel only as far as you can safely see. To be most efficient, take as big a step as possible and move your ax and one foot at the same time. Taking large steps will mean moving your ax every time you take a step. Remember to keep your heels flat.

Holding your ax in the self-arrest position prevents your hands from being able to "walk" down the slope. This becomes irrelevant when you are moving efficiently and get into a rhythm with your hands and feet. On a steep slope (where plunge stepping is not advised) with very soft snow, a proficient climber can modify the above technique and slide down the slope in the self-arrest position (see Chapter 5) to quickly lose some altitude. Be very careful so you stay in control. Other options for holding the ax include high dagger, *piolet manche*, and low dagger. The overhead swing with one or two axes is the slowest of these techniques but may be your best option on frozen ground.

### Pros

- It provides the best security on steep, firm snow.
- You are already in the self-arrest position if you fall.
- You can move quickly on steep, frozen snow.

### Cons

- It is difficult to see below you.
- Your hands may get cold and wet because they are in constant contact with the snow.
- Front-pointing is tiring and difficult in soft boots.

## ZIGZAGGING OR SIDESTEPPING

As the angle decreases, using the edges of your boot to create steps may feel more secure than front-pointing. Just like sidestepping while ascending, for descending you can descend straight down the fall line or make long zigzags. If you stand sideways on the slope, one foot will use its inside edge (big toe side), the other foot will use its outside edge (little toe side) against the snow. Descending diagonally is much more

difficult than ascending diagonally; the firmness of the snow will require you to kick your feet in different ways. In softer snow you can kick the inside or outside edge of your boot as you did for ascending (see Chapter 2). On firmer snow it may be much more effective to create a step by "slapping" your foot against the snow, which means swinging your foot against the snow nearly perpendicular into it versus across it. Another option on firm snow is to stomp your foot downward and "shave" away at the snow to make a platform for your foot (Figure 4-1).

To descend straight down sidestepping, maintain an out-of-balance stance (downhill foot forward, uphill foot back) the entire time you descend and choose one of the three techniques for making a step listed above. It is very likely that each foot will use a different technique! Descending while facing forward and sidestepping on firm snow is difficult. It sounds awkward, but it can be much easier to follow a diagonal path and walk backward down the slope kicking steps just as you did while ascending; do this only as long as necessary because your view behind you is restricted.

On lower angle slopes with soft snow, expend less energy by edging with your foot and letting it slide until it catches. Be flexible and creative.

Hold your ax using the self-arrest grip and the cane grip on lower-angle slopes, and high dagger and the self-arrest position on steeper slopes. Challenge yourself to keep your weight over your feet; if you lean in to the slope too far you are more likely to fall.

**Pros**

■ Sidestepping is easier on your calves.

**Cons**

■ Stepping down to kick your outside edge into the snow is tiring when following a steep angle.

## PLUNGE STEPPING (THE GORILLA STEP)

Standing up and facing outward while descending provides the best perspective for following a safe route. When to use the plunge step should be determined by the firmness of the snow more than the slope angle. When the snow is too soft for crampons, plunge stepping should be your primary means of descent. Outdoor educators refer to this technique as the gorilla step because it provides a nice image of what the technique looks like (Photo 4-4). Face downhill, feet shoulder-width apart, and knees slightly bent. Keeping your knees bent helps prevent hyperextension of your knee if you posthole. Let gravity do the work! Bring each foot down hard and dig your heel into the snow; your heel should be the first thing that makes contact with the snow. Always make your own path

*Photo 4-4. Plunge stepping is an efficient and safe way to descend steeper slopes with softer snow. Make sure you maintain an upright position so your weight stays over your feet.*

instead of using another person's because compressing the snow as you plunge helps control your speed and balance.

As you descend, hold the ice ax in the self-arrest grip because the main function of your ax is to help you stop if you slip. On most slopes your hands should be out to your sides to increase balance; your ax is not in the snow. Hold the ax in either hand when going straight down. The uphill hand is preferable when angling downslope. To ensure that you can stop quickly if you slip, hold the ice ax in the self-arrest position (one hand on the head, one hand at the base of the shaft, and held diagonally across your chest). This allows you to stop faster if you fall, but it prevents you from using the spike for balance. Holding your ax like this should be the exception, not the norm.

The most common reason people fall using this technique is because they lean too far back. The best position for your body is straight over your feet. It may feel safer to lean back, but it actually makes you more prone to falling because your heels hit the snow at a more glancing angle.

Just as front-pointing is tiring on your calves in firm snow, plunge stepping is tiring for your shins if your heels barely dig in. Modify the plunge step for more security by using a combination technique and plunge stepping with one foot and stomping the little toe side of the other foot on the slope to shave away at the snow to make a step (Photo 4-5). You can also lean down and plunge the shaft of your ax deep into the snow as you did for the self-belay while ascending.

Photo 4-5. Descending steep, firm snow may require plunging your ax and employing a combination technique for your feet.

### Pros
- You can move securely and see the route below.
- In soft snow you can descend quickly.

### Cons
- If your feet slip out from under you, you may take a hard fall on your bum and start sliding very quickly.
- It is more tiring and slower than glissading.

*Photo 4-6. The heel-n-side technique is used when heading diagonally down the slope and combines edging with your uphill foot and plunging with your downhill foot.*

### THE HEEL-N-SIDE: HALF SIDESTEPS AND HALF HEEL, FOR ANGLING DOWNWARD

Plunge stepping is effective because your weight helps drive your narrow heel into the snow, but it is awkward as a means of angling downhill. On lower-angle slopes and in snow that has only a few inches of soft snow, use the heel-n-side to move quickly along a path that does more traversing than descending. This is another combination technique because you kick the outside edge of one foot into the snow and plunge the heel of your downhill leg into the slope so your toes are pointing outward (Photo 4-6). Maintain a constant speed. In doing so, the spike of your ax does little more than help you maintain balance. Hold the ax in the self-arrest grip or the cane grip.

**Pros**
■ It is a fast method for angling down semi-firm snow.

**Cons**
■ You may be more prone to slipping if you encounter an area of snow that is too firm.

## CRAMPONS: TECHNIQUES FOR DESCENDING

Crampons provide excellent traction and make descending frozen snow much easier than kicking steps. However, they can also slow you down at times. When traveling down softer snow, plunge stepping without crampons is faster and safer. When the conditions are right, glissading (see below) is faster as well. Glissading with crampons is dangerous and not recommended.

The following techniques start with those generally used for steeper terrain and progress to those used on lower-angle slopes.

### FRONT-POINTING

Front-pointing is your most secure means of descent on steep ground. Facing in and descending is a slow process for inexperienced climbers, but with practice it should become your fastest way of descending firmer snow.

Hold the ax in high dagger, *piolet manche*, low dagger, or self-arrest position. The overhead swing with one or two axes is the slowest of these techniques, but it may be your best option on frozen ground. Remember to keep your heels low. See "Downhill Step Techniques" earlier in this chapter for tips on moving more quickly.

### Pros
- It loses the most elevation per step.
- It takes the shortest line toward an objective directly below you.
- Facing directly into the slope allows you to lean your arms against your ax, which takes weight off your legs.

### Cons
- It is more tiring on your calves.
- Facing into the slope reduces your ability to see below you.

### THE COMBINATION TECHNIQUE, THE AMERICAN TECHNIQUE, *PIED TROISIÈME*, OR THE THREE O'CLOCK POSITION

On steep slopes, a flat-footed technique becomes more difficult. The combination technique is simply front-pointing with one foot and using the French technique with your other foot. It is a compromise between security and energy expenditure. Kicking your front points with one foot gives you security; flat footing (the French technique) with the other saves energy.

Using this technique with very stiff leather boots or plastic mountaineering boots will require you to place your feet at more of a four o'clock and eight o'clock configuration. (See Photo 2-11.)

### THE FRENCH TECHNIQUE, *PIED À PLAT*

The French technique basically involves stomping or pushing your foot into the snow so your downward facing points stick in the snow. Use these flat-footed techniques when the angle of the slope allows it. A flat-footed technique should generally be your primary foot technique for descending with crampons. Remember to roll your ankle so you keep all the crampon points on the snow. On steeper slopes keeping your body weight over your feet is essential. Practice this to become proficient on steeper slopes. If the snow is soft, following a strict flat-footed technique is unnecessary. You can keep the sole of your boot horizontal and engage only one row of your points by stomping or kicking a step.

On the steepest slopes use the French technique to take a low-angle or a steep diagonal path down the slope. This is slower than the following techniques but offers better security, especially when you take small steps. Hold the ax in the high dagger, *piolet ramasse*, or the self-arrest grip with the spike used for balance.

### THE DUCK STEP, DUCK WALK, OR *PIED EN CANARD*

The duck step is merely a variation on the French technique and should be your standard mode of descent on moderate slopes (Photo 4-7). Stiff mountaineering boots will perform better when using the

*Photo 4-7. Descending with the duck step*

duck step for descending versus ascending. Unlike using the duck step when ascending, it is of no benefit to straddle a narrow ridge of snow with your feet.

Stand up straight with your knees slightly bent, and hold your arms out to the side for balance while holding your ax in the self-arrest grip. Self-arresting if you fall and slide is unlikely, but it may be possible to fall into the self-arrest position with your pick and crampon spikes in the snow. On the steepest slopes you can crouch down and use your ax in the self-arrest grip or use *piolet ramasse*.

Because the points on your crampons run parallel to your feet, walking straight down as the snow softens may cause your feet to slide out from under you. Using the duck step turns your feet more sideways so the wider side of your points are oriented downhill and so reduces your chances of sliding. As the angle of the snow continues to decrease, continue a "cowboy down" style by employing a slight duck walk and wider stance to avoid catching your crampons on your other leg.

### PIOLET RAMPE

*Piolet rampe* is another of the early European techniques for descending steeper slopes in a flat-footed manner, and should be reserved for short steep sections. While descending with your toes facing down hill or in the duck step, swing your ax as far ahead of you as is comfortable, making sure that your pick sticks very firmly in the snow (Photo 4-8). Squat down and move your feet forward while keeping your weight over your feet. (See Photos 4-9 and 4-10.) By pulling up and leveraging your ax, you prevent yourself from falling forward. The word *rampe* means *banister*, as in sliding your hand along the shaft (or banister/railing). Sliding your hand toward the head of the ax makes removing it from the snow easier and allows you to descend farther between swings. When you have

*Photo 4-8, top left. The first step in piolet rampe is to firmly swing your ax into the firm snow.*

*Photo 4-9, top right. Next, walk your feet down the slope while sliding your hand down the shaft as you continue to pull upward.*

*Photo 4-10, bottom right. Continue walking down as far as you can before moving your ax again.*

(Photos by Robert Buswold)

moved as far as is comfortable, reverse your pull on the ax so the pick comes out easily.

Attempting this technique on soft snow or ice or when your pick fails to penetrate will lead to failure. This technique works best with a classically curved pick because as you leverage the ax the teeth dig into the snow; a reverse-curved pick tends to slide out.

## GLISSADING

To glissade means to slide down snow in a seated, crouching, or standing position using your ax to help control your speed. It can be a fun reward after a day of climbing, but it can be dangerous. Glissading is usually much faster than walking, and when you need to lose elevation quickly it may be worth the risks involved.

A safe glissade requires adequate terrain and proper technique. The safest slope will have soft snow, a shape that allows you to see your entire route, an angle that gradually decreases at the bottom, and a runout free of rocks. The slope should also be free of protruding rocks. The perfect slope rarely exists so you must take precautions. If you are unsure about your ability to control your speed and stop, go slowly and practice self-arresting from the beginning. If you cannot see the entire route, descend in "pitches." This means that before you start, choose a stopping location where you can reassess. Never glissade farther than you can see. When you reach that point, stop and plan the next "pitch" from there. If time is not a concern and you are traveling in a group, one member can go first to scout the route for any hazards. Refrain from glissading all together if falling into a crevasse is a possibility.

Always consider why you are glissading. Thinking like a climber means considering what the consequences of your actions will be on yourself and your group. What you do during a big trip and what you do on a snowy slope near the car may look very different. Choose to glissade based on the conditions, not on convenience or desire. One of the worst reasons to glissade is because you are exhausted and think that glissading is an easy way to get down. Stopping or maintaining your speed on a steep slope (especially with a heavy pack after a long day) can be very difficult. When in doubt, it is safer to walk down. In fact, maintaining a constant and rhythmic pace may be faster and use less energy than constantly alternating between glissading and walking.

Once you have decided to glissade, follow these guidelines. Dress appropriately: Shell or softshell pants and gloves are essential. Remove your crampons! This is critical. Glissading with crampons is a recipe for broken ankles and legs. Maintain a safe speed so you can self-arrest if the snow conditions change. Store your equipment inside your pack (not on the outside) to avoid losing things.

Choose your glissading speed and technique based on your goal. If it has been a long day and glissading down a long, low-angle slope will save you time and energy, go slower by using a seated position and dig your heels and spike in more. To help maintain a slower speed, move out of the "trough" created by other climbers and make your own path; rougher snow has more friction.

### CHOOSING BETWEEN A SEATED OR STANDING TECHNIQUE

It takes less energy to sit down than stay standing, but a seated glissade down a steep slope is hard work for your arms and legs. A seated position allows you to control your speed better when you are just learning. Experienced climbers may find standing to be easier and faster.

A standing position offers better visibility and will allow you to see hazards such as rocks much sooner than while sitting. Additionally, standing is easier on your clothing and equipment; repeatedly sliding down slopes of firm snow will wear holes in your pants and your backpack.

Another issue to consider is possible injuries. Pockets of unconsolidated snow are inevitable, and hitting these with your backside is typically less injurious than plunging into one feet-first. Sliding over a rock may cause a bad laceration on your backside, which may be preferable to a broken leg. Falling while standing may cause a jarring injury, and if you fail to arrest quickly you may lose control.

### SEATED GLISSADE

Start by sitting in the snow and kicking your heels in so you do not slide. If you are nervous or your skills are rusty, mentally review how to control your speed and self-arrest before you begin sliding. Hold the head of your ax using the self-arrest grip; grab the shaft with your other hand a few inches up from the spike. Control your speed by pushing the spike into the snow next to you (Photo 4-11). This technique is easier if you keep your arms straight so that your body weight does a lot of the work. Rotate your hand on the head so that your pick faces sideways, not downward and into

Photo 4-11. To control your speed in a seated glissade, dig in your heels and the spike of your ax. For additional force, this climber could straighten her right arm and let her body weight push the spike into the snow.

your leg. Put your legs together and straight in front of you. Dig your heels in to slow down; lift them up to go faster. You can also use the pick to control your speed by pushing it in the snow. If you start going too fast, it is best to come to a complete stop by rolling over and self-arresting.

You can also control your speed by assuming a position similar to that shown in Photo 5-3 in the next chapter. Use a paddling motion to keep yourself moving when you start to slow down.

Popular routes may have a groove or trough worn smooth by people glissading in the same fall line. This path can be advantageous when the natural slope is uncomfortably bumpy and when the angle of the slope decreases because you can slide farther. These paths can also be dangerous because rolling out of them to self-arrest may be impossible, and on a busy day, out-of-control people might crash into you from behind.

On hot summer days the snow may be so soft that you start a miniature wet slide avalanche. If it stays small, it can be great fun to ride on this blob of snow between your legs. These become hazardous when they grow too large for you to control your speed and you ride them into hazardous terrain below.

## STANDING GLISSADE (BOOT SKIING)

Boot skiing is my favorite technique for descending, second of course to actual skiing. Safe and efficient boot skiing means finding the right angle for your body and your heels, just like plunge stepping. Stand up straight with your knees slightly bent and hold your arms out to your side for balance while holding your ax in the self-arrest grip (not the cane grip). (See Photo 4-12.) While leaning back toward the slope digs your heels in more, leaning too far back will cause your feet to slip out from under you. Leaning forward and digging your heels in less will allow you to go faster or to keep going when the slope angle

decreases. Leaning forward too much may cause you to fall forward if you hit an area of increased friction. Another concern is plunging your feet into a section of soft snow or an elephant trap, and falling and sliding out of control. It is essential to keep looking downslope.

Modifying this technique so that one foot is more downhill than another (kind of like telemark skiing) will give you better balance, but you also will not travel nearly as far. On the steepest slopes, it is easier and safer to go down while facing sideways (like snowboarding), but you should switch back to the unmodified technique to slide the farthest.

You can control your speed by changing the amount your heels dig in and by attempting to carve turns. If the snow is firm and you have enough momentum you can push off of one foot repeatedly to alter your course slightly. Stopping is accomplished by increasing the amount your heels dig in or by turning sideways and digging the uphill sides of your boots into the snow. This motion is similar to stopping while skiing or doing a "hockey stop" on ice skates.

If you are going straight down it should not matter which hand you hold your ax in, but if you are following any kind of diagonal path, hold your ax in the uphill hand. Keeping your ax in one hand (self-arrest grip) allows you to maintain better balance. When approaching a hazard, switch to holding the ax with both hands in the self-arrest position in case you fall. However, holding the ax with both hands

*Photo 4-12. Boot ski with your toes pointed straight downhill and your arms out to the side for balance.*

should be minimized to help you maintain balance.

Lower on the mountain the angle decreases and the snow gets softer. If you want to maximize your glissading, switch to the seated glissade because it allows you to travel farther and is less dangerous if you encounter a pocket of soft snow.

The crouching (or "3-point") form looks just like it sounds. It offers no distinct advantage. Crouching instead of standing fails to save energy and reduces your ability to see down the slope. To keep it simple, choose between sitting and standing.

Glissading without an ax is not recommended. However, if you are already proficient moving on snow and you encounter a low-angle slope of soft snow with a safe runout, sliding down might be safe. Glissading may also be the right choice for escaping an impending thunderstorm. Ski poles, a stick, a long narrow rock, or even your tent poles may be used. While seated, grab the base of the poles with one hand and 2–3 feet higher with the other hand. Keeping your arms straight and comfortably far apart gives you leverage to push

the tip of your poles into the snow. Because these objects are no substitute for an ax, it is better to descend more slowly by digging in your feet as well. Self-arresting will also be more difficult, so make sure your choice to glissade without an ax is an appropriate one.

When descending as a group, spreading out as you glissade reduces the chances of members running into each other, but in a bowl, your fall lines will eventually merge. If you are all sliding down the same path, leave adequate room between members to avoid collisions.

## THE KICK AND GLIDE

This technique is your last attempt at putting gravity to work on the descent. It is really just an intermediate step between boot skiing and simply walking downhill. The motion of this technique is very similar to the diagonal stride used while cross-country skiing. To do this, just before you come to a halt boot skiing, push off with one foot so your other foot can slide along the snow; repeat as long as possible. Maintain an upright body position and keep looking forward to avoid pockets of unconsolidated snow.

# Chapter 5

While climbing on this early winter snow is straightforward, ice lurking near the surface and a boulder field at the bottom mean the climber must take care to avoid falling.

# Self-Arresting

*"The best defense is a good offense."*

Up until this point in the book, the skills discussed have focused on preventing a fall down a snow slope. If you fall you must be able to stop yourself. To self-arrest means to stop sliding or prevent yourself from sliding if you fall. Most often this means forcing the pick of your ax into the snow and digging your toes in to slow yourself as your pick and feet dig into and scrape at the snow. Self-arresting should be considered a viable option for stopping yourself if you start sliding on soft snow up to an angle of 40 degrees. In general, as the slope angle increases, the snow must continue to soften for you to increase your likelihood of a successful arrest. This is because softer snow will allow your ice ax to cut through the snow to gradually slow yourself. Self-arresting generally fails to work on firm snow because once your pick sticks into the

snow (if it sticks it all), it is unable to cut through the snow. If you are moving quickly, as soon as your pick sticks in the snow the muscles of your arms must absorb all the force of your body instantly. Because this tends to be impossible, you lose your grip on your ax and let go. The only viable option for self-arresting on firm snow, no matter what the angle, is to fall into the correct self-arrest position before you start sliding.

Overestimating your ability to self-arrest is a common mistake. Knowing your limitations is critical for respecting the mountain. Knowing how to self-arrest provides great mental security that allows you to enjoy traveling on lower-angle terrain because you know you can stop yourself if you fall. The skill of self-arresting is a lot like insurance: You need it and you should rarely have to use it.

To deal with the consequences of falling on snow, practice falling in the same types of conditions you plan to climb. The best place to practice self-arresting is on a short slope with a clean runout, free of rocks and other hazards.

The goal of self-arresting is to stop as quickly as possible. The techniques outlined below are the most efficient means of stopping yourself for some "classic" scenarios, but in the end the true measure of your arrest is whether you stopped or not.

## THE BASICS OF SELF-ARRESTING

Photo 5-1 shows the final position you should be in when self-arresting, no matter how you fall. With your head upslope, pull your arms in tight so the weight of your torso is over your ax. If your arms extend above your head you have less control of your ax and can dislocate your shoulders. Turn your head away so your adze does not poke you in the face. Keep your butt high in the air to help put your weight over your ax and your feet. Spread your feet apart to reduce the chances of rolling over. In softer snow, aggressively kick your feet into the snow because your stopping power comes from your ax and your feet combined.

A word of caution: Assuming the self-arrest position does not guarantee you will stop where you want, if at all. If you have fallen and continue sliding after assuming the ideal body position it is time for more drastic measures. Dig your ax in harder or even jump and slam your ax and feet into the snow like your life depends on it…because it just might. Take learning this

*Photo 5-1. The ideal self-arrest position for someone with an ice ax, but without crampons.*

skill seriously; too often beginners give up during an attempt if they drop their ax or initially fail to stop while trying to self-arrest.

## SELF-ARRESTING WITHOUT AN ICE AX

Stopping quickly is essential because in most cases your speed is only going to increase. Photo 5-2 shows the ideal self-arrest position for someone without an ax. The only difference between this position and the self-arrest position with an ax is that you dig your elbows in the snow to stop yourself. If the snow is soft you can try interlocking your fingers and pressing your forearms and hands against the snow,

essentially turning your forearms into a snowplow. Reality check: In firm snow arresting this way is nearly impossible.

If you fail to stop yourself, prepare to deal with the hazards below you. If you are headed toward a boulder field, keeping your body flat against the snow reduces your chances of being propelled forward after hitting the first obstacle and cartwheeling through the boulders. The drawback is that you will feel a greater force from the single object you encounter. Try to hit an object with a glancing blow instead of straight on.

When sliding toward a crevasse or gap in the snow, try to jump over this void. Do this by sliding in a seated position with your legs tucked up near your butt and your hands on the snow. Just before you get to the lip, push up with your hands and lean your body forward so your weight is over your feet. Now jump. You will be going much faster when you land, but this may be much better than falling to your death. Reality check: Attempting to do this while sliding fast on frozen ground may be impossible.

## SELF-ARRESTING WITH AN ICE AX

Before you consider what technique to use if you fall, ask yourself if stopping yourself is realistic. If the snow is so hard that your pick cannot penetrate it, stopping will be impossible. Either accept this risk, avoid this terrain, climb on it only if the consequences of falling are minimal, or use additional aids (crampons, multiple ice axes, ropes, etc.).

If the snow is firm enough that the pick of your ice ax will penetrate the snow but will not cut through the snow if you pull downward, you may only have one chance to stop yourself. If you fall on this type of snow your goal is to land in a position where your pick penetrates the snow and your arms are bent so that you can absorb the shock of falling without sliding. If you fail to self-arrest here, stopping yourself may be impossible.

When the snow is soft enough that your pick can penetrate and slice through the snow and you can jab in your feet as well, your self-arrest should be successful.

## SLIPPING WHILE STANDING UP AND FACING THE SLOPE

If your feet slip while you are facing the slope, fall into the self-arrest position with your pick in the snow; alternately, plunge

*Photo 5-2. The ideal self-arrest position for someone without an ice ax or crampons*

Photo 5-3. This climber is rolling to her left side to get her pick into the snow as soon as possible.

Photo 5-4. After her pick is in the snow she rolls over into the self-arrest position.

the spike of your ax into the snow as you would for the self-belay. (See Photos 3-9 and 3-10 in Chapter 3.)

## BACK AGAINST THE SNOW AND FEET FACING DOWNHILL

In Photos 5-3 and 5-4 notice how the person is rolling to the same side as the pick of the ice ax. It is possible to roll to the other side and put your pick in the snow, but this takes more time.

Photos 5-5 and 5-6 illustrate why trying to self-arrest with the spike of your ax usually ends in failure if you are sliding. Having your hand on the head leverages the ax out of the snow.

Photo 5-5. *Attempting to stab the spike of your ax into the snow to self-arrest may seem like a good idea...*

Photo 5-6. *...but the problem is that as you slide, you leverage the ax out of the snow.*

Photo 5-7. When sliding headfirst on your belly the first step is to put your ice ax out to your side.

Photo 5-8. When your ax digs into the snow the drag created on one side will swing your feet around.

Photo 5-9. The last step is to get into the ideal self-arrest position.

## CHEST AGAINST THE SNOW AND HEAD DOWNHILL

This situation could occur if you fall forward while walking downhill or fall forward when bending over at a rest stop.

By sticking your ice ax out to the side, as shown in Photos 5-7 and 5-8, you create drag on one side, which swings your legs around in the opposite direction. Once your feet are below you, assume the self-arrest position (Photo 5-9). Practicing this technique is much easier if someone holds your feet as you position yourself on your belly before sliding.

## BACK AGAINST THE SNOW AND HEAD DOWNHILL

This situation may occur if you lean back too far or catch your heel while stepping backward. Practicing this technique is easier if someone holds your feet as you position yourself on your back before sliding.

Stick your ax out to the side, as shown in Photos 5-10 and 5-11, to create drag on one side, which swings your legs around in the opposite direction and simultaneously puts you on your belly. Once your head is up and facing the slope, assume the self-arrest position.

If the head of your ax is in your right hand and your legs are off to the right side, the above techniques will not work. In this or any other peculiar situation, roll over as best you can and follow the steps for one of the techniques listed above.

*Photo 5-10. If you start on your back and with your head facing downhill, plant the pick of your ax off to one side.*

*Photo 5-11. After your legs swing around, get into the self-arrest position.*

*Photo 5-12. The ideal self-arrest position for someone with an ice ax and crampons*

## SELF-ARRESTING WHILE WEARING CRAMPONS

Sliding, intentionally or unintentionally, while wearing crampons is not advised. With good climbing technique a fall that leads to a slide should almost never happen. On firm snow, the main cause of falling is tripping over crampon spikes by dragging your feet or catching them on your other leg. If this happens, immediately fall into the self-arrest position and jab your pick and your front points into the snow. If you fail to self-arrest and begin to slide, stopping will become exponentially more difficult. If you attempt to dig your crampons into the snow while sliding, the spikes may catch in the snow and severely twist your ankle, cause you to flip over, or both. The correct position for self-arresting with crampons is the same as without crampons, except that you lift up your feet and dig your knees into the snow (Photo 5-12).

Another reason people fall while wearing crampons is that snow accumulates under their feet and prevents their points from gripping the snow. Self-arresting in these soft snow conditions will generally be easier. If your crampons do not gain purchase while climbing, they may not while sliding either, decreasing your chance of injuring yourself.

## SELF-ARRESTING WHILE WEARING A BACKPACK

When you take a fall wearing a backpack you might roll to either side or tumble head over heels. The goal is to get into the self-arrest position no matter which direction you have to roll to get there. If you get caught on your back with your feet uphill, spin yourself over onto your belly. If you start rolling you will have quite a bit of momentum, so stopping will be more difficult. Spreading your legs, straightening your body, and changing your orientation (lying parallel to the slope) can improve your chances of gaining control. When you get into the self-arrest position, keep your feet wider than normal and your belly closer to the snow to help prevent rolling onto your back or side.

If you practice climbing and self-arresting while wearing a big pack on steep snow you will be more confident and better prepared to deal with a real fall should it happen. To practice, bring your backpack and some stuff sacks along for a peak climb. You can get the feel for a heavy backpack by filling some stuff sacks with snow to simulate all the gear you might carry during an expedition.

## SELF-ARRESTING USING SKI POLES

Knowing how to self-arrest with ski poles while kicking steps, or while using skis, a splitboard, or snowshoes, is essential. A fall may occur while traversing from soft snow onto hard snow, while traveling on a firm slope that gradually gets steeper, or even while just walking on a well-worn path or on steps kicked by others if the path or steps are icy. You need to be aware of and recognize a transition zone before it becomes a problem.

To self-arrest with ski poles, start by lying on your side (Photo 5-13). If your hands are not through the wrist straps (and they shouldn't be if you're in avalanche terrain), grab your poles near the base and pull in tight so the poles tuck between your elbow and ribs. With your other hand, hold the pole much higher so you have better leverage to keep the tip perpendicular to the snow. If your hand is through the wrist strap, you will be forced to keep your hand on the grip. If you're wearing skis or snowshoes, dig their edges in. If you're wearing boots, kick your toes into the snow and face the snow.

*Photo 5-13. The correct self-arrest position for someone wearing skis while carrying ski poles*

# Chapter 6

*After having climbed up your intended line of descent, you will have a better idea of what to expect from the snow conditions when descending.*

# Traversing, Resting, and Other Skills

*"It's not always how fast you climb, but how much time you spend stopping."*

## TRAVERSING

Moving horizontally in the mountains is just as important as going up or down. When climbing a narrow ridge it may be easier to traverse below the ridge than to "tightrope walk" your way across the top, especially in the wind. While you may not be gaining elevation, you will be moving in the direction of the summit. Traversing is important when crossing a snow slope that is prone to rockfall. Take the shortest path, even if it means losing a little bit of elevation, to get out of the bowling alley as fast as possible.

### FRONT-POINTING

As with ascending straight up a slope, reserve front-pointing for steeper slopes when you need maximum security. Shuffling your feet is generally preferable to crossing one foot in front of the other on steep terrain. For additional balance, lean your knees against the snow while you move your ax. Two basic shuffling techniques exist:

1. Take large steps with your leading foot and kick your trailing foot as close to it as possible.
2. Kick small steps with your leading foot and place your trailing foot in the step left behind.

Options for holding the ax while traversing include high dagger, *piolet manche*, low dagger, self-belay, and self-arrest position. The overhead swing with one or two axes is the slowest of these techniques but may be your best option on frozen terrain.

One common technique is to "crab crawl" across a slope by front-pointing and having an ax in each hand. This is likely to be your fastest means of traversing on difficult snow.

*Photo 6-1. Front-pointing across the slope with the ice ax in the leading hand*

**Pros**

■ It allows you to move quickly because front-pointing is a secure means of travel.

**Cons**

■ Shuffling your feet across the slope is tiring.

### SIDESTEPPING

This is the same technique as sidestepping (described in Chapter 2 on Ascending). Hold your ice ax using the self-arrest grip, *piolet canne*, self-belay, self-arrest position, or high dagger. In softer snow, angling your feet (especially your downhill foot) slightly inward will produce a modified front-pointing technique and give you more security. In very firm snow, it may be more effective to "slap" your foot nearly perpendicular to the snow to produce an edge to stand on.

**Pros**

■ Each leg does equal work kicking steps.

**Cons**

■ It is awkward if you lose elevation as you traverse.

### TRAVERSING WITH CRAMPONS

Using crampons to move across a slope is similar to kicking steps. On low-angle slopes, use the French technique and step one foot in front of the other to move faster and maintain a better view of your route. Reserve front-pointing for the steepest slopes. Prevent your points from catching on your other leg by shuffling your feet.

### RESTING

Resting efficiently is an important skill. When you stop and rest, expend as little energy as possible so your muscles actually rest. Look for places to rest that require minimal snow excavation and allow you to stand without having to use your ax. Finding a place to sit on an open slope is unlikely, but these occasionally exist near (and on) rock outcrops.

*Photo 6-2. Pausing in-balance allows you to support your weight with your skeleton instead of your muscles.*

How often and for how long you rest is up to personal and group preference. When the climbing is monotonous, take a quick break when you change directions or get to a landmark (e.g., pebble on the snow), between verses of a song, or once you have made a certain number of steps. If you are very tired you may only make five steps between breaks; if you are feeling stronger, count more. As boring as this sounds, counting steps and breaths to limit your breaks is an effective way to keep you going.

## THE REST STEP

The rest step consists of ending any set of steps on snow (or on the trail) with a straight leg (usually standing in-balance) so you can take a momentary rest and let your weight be supported by your skeleton, not your muscles (Photo 6-2). This is an effective way to take short breaks when a longer break is not advised.

## THE HIGH STEP REST

This technique is used when zigzagging on slopes when the snow is soft and falling is not

*Photo 6-3. The high step rest is a way of varying your resting stances.*

*Photo 6-4. To begin climbing again, kick your right foot at a comfortable height and then step up with your left foot into the precut step.*

a concern. The high step rest means ending a step out of balance, but instead of placing the forward foot in the position it would normally go when you continue moving, kick it into the location your back foot would go next (Photo 6-3). When you are ready to start climbing again, kick your forward foot into a comfortable position you can stand on (Photo 6-4). When you step up on this foot, your rear leg steps into the precut step. The key to this rest is kicking your upslope foot into the snow in the exact position where your other foot will go on its next step.

### THE ICE AX THRONE

If keeping your backside warm and dry is a priority, or you have plenty of time, this is a great technique for taking a sit-down break on a snow slope. Use this technique on slopes where falling is not a concern.

*Photo 6-5. A completed ice ax throne*

Make the ice axe throne (Photo 6-5) by cutting out a depression in the snow as wide as your hips. On the edges cut two small platforms for the ends of your ax to rest on. After you have knocked away any extra snow, sit down and kick your heels into the snow. It should only take half a minute or so to dig the right-sized seat, and it will be worth it.

### REMOVING YOUR PACK, SKIS, OR SNOWBOARD

Taking your pack off may cause you to slip, drop your pack, or both. Prepare yourself ahead of time by keeping snacks and other essentials in your pockets. Keep the rope or other climbing hardware easily accessible so your partner can remove it from your pack.

If you feel secure letting go of your ax, jab the shaft or pick into the snow and loop your shoulder strap over your ice ax or use a carabiner to attach them. Alternatively, create a depression with your feet or adze to set your pack into.

When carrying skis, a snowboard, or ski poles, be diligent about securing them so they will not slide away. Skis with straight tails should be pushed deep in the snow. A snowboard or skis without straight tails should be turned perpendicular to the slope and braced in place with your knees. Skis, snowboards, or ski poles can also be clipped to an ice ax.

### OTHER SKILLS

Adaptability is a big part of success in all walks of life but particularly when you're walking on snow. You need to be able to

Photo 6-6. To jump out onto the snow, aim toward a flat location.

Photo 6-7. Avoid losing your balance and sliding down the slope by landing in a stable position. Hold the ice ax in the self-arrest position so you can self-arrest quickly should you fall.

adjust to changes from rock to snow and back to rock again, and to be able to make adjustments not only to changing conditions but also missing equipment.

## TRANSITIONING FROM SNOW TO ROCK

Just when you thought the hard part was over, a large gap stands between the snow slope you are on and the rock buttress above. Always approach a melted out zone between rock and snow with caution. What seems like solid snow near the lip may be the cover over a large elephant trap. Look for a place where you can step directly onto the rock. Consider climbing down between the snow and rock if it is safe, and then transitioning to the rock. As you move onto the rock, kick the toe of your boot against the rock a few times to clear the snow.

## TRANSITIONING FROM ROCK TO SNOW

Just as "dynoing" or jumping for a hand-hold while rock climbing involves the risk of falling, jumping from rock onto snow of unknown hardness can be risky. Leaping becomes more hazardous when you are tired, your pack is heavy, your view is obscured by clouds, or a combination of the three. If you are unsure of the snow's firmness, throw a rock at it. Whether you plan to land on flat ground or a slope, land so that you have the best chance of maintaining your balance and falling into the self-arrest position if needed. (See Photos 6-6 and 6-7.)

When walking on low-angle terrain over a boulder field or flat rock outcrop, expect the snow nearest the rock to be soft. Your concern, especially in a boulder field, is plunging in and twisting a joint or hitting your leg against the rock. Make the transition onto snow by leaping as far out from the rocks as possible. Hold your ice ax in one hand to help you make the longest jump possible. Land as gently as possible and on both feet at once to reduce your chance of breaking through the snow.

If jumping seems too risky because you know you are going to sink in, it may be best to intentionally break through the snow next to the boulders and then posthole to solid snow. If the boulder field covered in soft snow is long, consider crawling on your hands and knees and using your ice ax (or sticks or ski poles) as snowshoes for your hands.

### LEARNING FROM EXPERIENCE: TEST BEFORE YOU LEAP

The benefit of being optimistic while climbing is that when faced with obstacles you have the mindset that it will work out fine if you keep going and so perhaps save yourself from wasting time looking for another way. The drawback to optimism is going too far before realizing you should have turned around a while ago and now you are doing something you should not.

While traveling around Silver Star Mountain in Washington, I went to scout the next day's route. I thought our snowfield would be visible at a pass between two cirques, but it was not. I decided to downclimb some rock into the bowl and then slide down some snow to see our gully. The farther down I climbed, the less I wanted to climb back up. When my rock scrambling options ended, I decided to leap over a gap and onto the snow slope below. I threw a few small pebbles at the snow to help me assess the snow's firmness. The leap went well and I oriented my body so that one foot was ahead of the other. However, the snow was firmer than I had predicted, and I landed leaning too far back. Luckily the slope below was gentle enough to justify the leap—and I had plenty of room to self-arrest.

Conclusion: I should have scrambled back up and found a bigger stone to test the snow. Had I done this, I would have realized the snow was harder than I thought and then I would have leaned forward more on my landing so I would have boot skied down the slope as planned.

**LEARNING FROM EXPERIENCE: CUTTING STEPS IN THE SHADE**

A few years back in Colorado's Gore Range, I was trying to catch up with some friends during the late summer. From my vantage point on a ridge, scrambling along the ridge seemed better than descending into the valley and hiking up to the pass where they were headed. On the way I encountered a small section of ice with a few rocks sticking out on the north-facing side of a small peak. Not wanting to retreat, I picked up the best rock I could find and began using it to chop steps in the ice. I was backpacking so I did not have an ax and I was wearing a T-shirt, shorts, and no gloves. My plan was working brilliantly until I moved into the shade. Then I got quite cold, but turning back or taking my pack off was not an option. I stayed calm and made it across, and I learned a valuable lesson. Although I did a good job of picking the best route and choosing an appropriate rock to cut steps with, I failed to put on gloves and a jacket because I did not notice that some of the route was in the shade.

## WHAT IF YOU DO NOT HAVE AN ICE AX?

When caught without an ice ax in the high country you have a couple options. To make adequate steps or stop a severe fall, find the longest, pointiest, but lightest rock you can. The best rock will resemble a wedge-shaped piece of pizza or a dagger. Cut steps as you would with an ice ax. To self-arrest, grip the rock in a way that gives you the best chance of keeping the pointy end perpendicular to the snow.

Ski poles or a walking stick provide little more than balance on firm snow. If you do fall and your hands are not through the wrist straps, grab your pole near the base and pull in tight so the pole tucks between your elbow and ribs (Photo 5-13). With your other hand, hold the pole much higher so you have better leverage to keep the tip perpendicular to the snow. If your hand is through the wrist strap, you will be forced to keep your hand on the grip. If wearing only boots, kick your toes into the snow. Remember, kicking steps is the main way to protect yourself. If you are without an ax, take the time to kick steps to prevent yourself from slipping. If a snowy trail is frozen, it is usually easier to kick your own steps in the undisturbed snow beside it.

## HOW TO AVOID POSTHOLING

Sometimes you will encounter areas where the snowpack is too soft to support your weight; however, even then by paying very close attention to the subtleties of the snow you can stay on top where others are breaking through.

Consider these tips the next time you are walking on soft, unsupportive snow:

- Take smaller steps and keep your feet flat to distribute your weight over a larger area.
- Consider using a stick or ski poles to help distribute your weight over a greater area.
- If all else fails, get down on your hands and knees and crawl to distribute your weight.

- Notice the texture and shade of the snow. The surface may look very sugary, crystalline, or more compacted. It may also have a darker or lighter shade to it. If one type of snow is unconsolidated, firm snow of another type may only be a step away.
- The sun is a major factor in warming the snow each day. Slopes or even small features that face more directly toward the sun soften faster. Look for subtle variations in the aspect of the snow so you can walk on snow that faces less directly toward the sun.
- In forests, stay as far as possible from standing or fallen trees, especially later in the day. Trees and rocks warm in the sun and emit infrared light. Snow absorbs infrared light very well and can soften quickly near a warm object. On the other hand, staying closer to trees allows you to stay on snow that is shaded and out of the sun.
- On low-angle slopes, following the path of tiny (but still covered) creeks often provides better snow than open slopes.
- Travel on the shady side of the valley (usually the north-facing slope) during the summer.
- If you know the snow is going to be soft, consider taking a slightly longer route to spend more time on dry ground.
- If you begin to posthole, angle your shin forward into the snow to decrease the distance you sink. Also, move your other foot forward so you can transfer some of your weight to it.
- Avoid low areas, especially where the willows can be seen poking through the snow. They are a good indicator of unconsolidated snow.

Traveling on breakable snow will bring some people to tears. Pay close attention to the appearance of the snow. When you have exhausted all of the techniques listed above, postholing may be your only option. When you reach this point, take the shortest route possible to your destination and avoid expending too much energy thrashing about and getting angry. Postholing can be exhausting, so share the workload between the group.

## PLANNING YOUR SNOW CLIMB

In late spring and early summer, especially after a big snow year, finding a slope that matches your abilities should be easy because most slopes are covered with snow. As the summer continues, the slopes that hold the snow most will be those that receive the least sunlight. On your approach to the climb, stop to plan your ascent at a location where you can see the entire route. Make a drawing or take a photo of the route if it will help you during the climb. Route-finding can be challenging when you are on the mountain because you have a limited view ahead. A gully that branches may look better in one direction, but you will not be able to tell if the snow continues around the bend. Reviewing a photo or drawing may help you stay on route.

Another helpful tip is to continually look down as you are climbing up so you know what the mountain will look like on your descent. This perspective can be essential when traveling on any medium, even a trail, because if you miss a junction and head the wrong way, you will recognize that the landscape looks different. Also look for notable landmarks (e.g., an interesting tree or peculiar natural feature) that you can find while descending.

## COMMUNICATION ON THE MOUNTAIN

"Left" and "right" are different directions depending on whether you are looking up or down a mountain. To alleviate confusion, when looking at a mountain speak about features being to "climber's left" or "climber's right." For example, "climb the main gully until it splits and take the route to climber's right." When descending or facing downhill, you would say, "skier's left" or "skier's right."

When the wind is blowing and members of a group are spread apart, communication may be difficult. If you are crossing a slope one at a time, you want to make sure the person who has just crossed is in a safe location and ready to watch you as you climb. A simple communication signal is to pat the top of your head with the palm of one of your hands to signify, "I'm okay." Moving as a group is fastest, but climbing one at a time is appropriate when you are concerned about avalanches, rockfall, or if one person is scouting ahead.

When you cannot see your partner, verbal communication needs to be simple and concise. If you and your partner are traveling one at a time through a section that ends with the leader out of sight, prepare ahead of time for this potential communication problem. A simple and concise call, such as "I'm safe," can be yelled by the leader so the second climber knows they can proceed.

Examine Photo 6-8, then contemplate the scenarios described below. On the approach to the couloirs, follow a path that keeps you away from potential rockfall from the steep buttress. The little bit of snow that has slid into the gully (indicated by the clean white snow) gives you a clear view of the fall line; stay to the right of this during the lower section. Exposed rock near the top of the left gully may indicate difficult climbing and rotten snow, but the righthand gully has a cornice.

If you are climbing the righthand gully, the dirty snow to the right of the white streak down the fall line is more out-of-the-way of rockfall. The consequence of climbing on the right means you are more exposed to rocks that fall from the large buttress. Sometimes climbing a gully means choosing the lesser of two evils, in this case choosing between staying in the bowling alley or staying near a cliff. Make your choice as to where to climb an intentional one. For example, if the previous night was cold, the cornice may be frozen and stable but rockfall may be an issue. If the previous night was warm, the unfrozen cornice may be your main concern.

If you are climbing the lefthand gully, the thin buttress separating the two gullies

*Photo 6-8. The Whine Couloirs in Colorado's Elk Mountains*

protects you from rocks falling down either one. It is difficult to determine which side of the gully would be best to climb. This is where you would use your judgment and make medium-scale routefinding decisions along the way.

The simplest descent from the summit would be to walk down the ridge toward the snow near the saddle. On a rounded ridge it is unlikely you will be able to see the best location for descending. Taking a photograph on the approach will be valuable later. Be careful transitioning from the talus to the snow; transition points are where accidents happen. On a warm day the snow may be unconsolidated next to the rocks and firm only a few feet downslope. Once you are on the snow, stay high and angle down to the "skier's right" to position yourself above the long clean slope of snow. Traversing first, instead of descending, prevents you from descending directly toward the cliffs below you. Descending straight down is easier than angling down, but taking an angle will prevent exposure to rockfall from the horizontal rock bands above. Once the route below you looks clear, start plunge stepping down the fall line. If you feel comfortable, glissade.

If your goal is to climb toward the saddle in the photo, zigzagging (the solid line in the photo) will be the most energy-efficient route. The path indicated on the photo stays below the exposed rocks. Alternating your directions works both of your arms and legs evenly. Climbing just to the right of the long horizontal outcrop allows you to have a close inspection as you pass by to inspect for a resting place. Once you have passed the outcrop, follow a path of ascent similar to the dashed line marking the descent.

These two routes mark the cleanest lines of ascent to gain the ridge. Once you are on the ridge, hiking to the summit is easiest along the ridge. In general, it is best to stay as far above a hazard below you as possible; if you fall, you have a longer distance over which to stop yourself. If the obstacle below you is a rocky ledge, it might be safest to walk on the rocks so falling is not an issue. If your route requires you to navigate between rock outcrops, it is safer to traverse below a rock than above it.

Even with a topo map, it can be difficult to determine how much elevation you have gained, especially if you are in a narrow gully. Besides using an altimeter, a great way to estimate your progress is to track your height relative to a nearby peak with a known elevation. Attempting to look across a valley and estimate a point of equal height without an aid is difficult. Do this accurately by holding your inclinometer level and looking along its edge toward your nearby peak. For example, if you estimate that your elevation is equal to that of the summit across the valley and that peak is 200 feet lower than the peak you are climbing, you are almost at the top. (See the avalanche section in Chapter 7 to learn how to use an inclinometer.)

Mountains always look steeper when you look straight at them. Before you decide that a distant slope appears too steep to climb, try this technique for visualizing its angle: Tilt your head 90 degrees so your head is horizontal and look at the slope. For whatever reason, this perspective will give you a better idea of how steep a slope is.

## ADDITIONAL CONSIDERATIONS FOR SKIERS AND SNOWBOARDERS

Lots of great skiing and snowboarding terrain is out of reach of ski lifts, helicopters, and regular ski touring. Many of the approaches to these more inaccessible places involve steep, firm snow. After the ski areas have closed and the summer snow has stabilized, the mountains are often in great shape for ski and snowboard descents. Early summer is the best time because without any new snow falling the snow surface is at first stable and smooth; however, as the summer rolls on the snow soon becomes pitted with depressions and grooves.

Although your skis, snowboard, and shovel can be used as aids during an ascent, they are no substitute for an ice

*Photo 6-9. Skis mounted diagonally on a pack*

ax. If you anticipate climbing firm snow, bring an ice ax.

For safety and to prepare for the descent, it is usually prudent to climb what you plan to ski or ride. It gives you the opportunity to look for hazards such as elephant traps or icy sections. If you climb the slope early in the morning, you can make your descent when the snow has softened enough for carving turns but is not so soft that there is a risk of wet-snow avalanches. Waiting until your route has been in the sun for a while may make kicking steps easier, but you may miss the ideal window for skiing.

Climbing what you plan to descend is not always a good idea, however. Wallowing up steep powder is no fun. Climbing your line of descent may also expose you to avalanche and rockfall hazards. In many

*Photo 6-10. Skis mounted in A-frame fashion with a strap at the top to keep the tails out-of-the-way of the climber's legs*

situations you are better off approaching along a ridge or another safe path.

Today's wider skins and better snowshoes allow travelers to climb steeper slopes, but this means the consequences of falling may be worse. As you are skinning or snowshoeing up a slope, the first important decision is when to remove the boards or snowshoes from your feet and carry them on your pack.

When to transition from skinning to carrying skis is partly a matter of personal preference and partly a matter of safety. Consider the snow below your feet. Are you likely to fall and what will happen if you do? The angle may have not changed, but the snow may now be so hard that your edges have trouble gripping. Keep assessing your route as you ascend. It may be easier and safer to transition lower in order to avoid a harrowing transition higher. Switching from skinning to climbing means putting your skis on your pack and getting out your ax.

If you plan to climb snow that requires an ice ax, it is important to have a backpack to accommodate your skis or board. If you are in avalanche terrain your backpack should accommodate a shovel, probe, and other safety gear. Skis are commonly carried vertically or diagonally. (See Photos 6-9 and 6-10). The disadvantage of having your skis vertical, using the A-frame method, is that they may hit the back of your legs as you climb; reduce this problem by using a strap to cinch the tips together, thus pulling the tails out of the way of your legs. Mounting your skis diagonally makes putting them on and

*Photo 6-11. A snowboard mounted vertically on a backpack*

taking them off your pack easier than the A-frame method. Be careful climbing with your skis mounted vertically or diagonally because if you bend over, the tips may bump into the snow, rocks, trees, or other people. A snowboard is typically mounted

*Photo 6-12. This technique for holding a snowboard while ascending a slope is only effective at holding a fall when the soft snow is deeper.*

*Photo 6-13. When climbing a slope with your skis in your hands hold the skis by their top sheets and push the edges into the snow. The skis will only keep you from sliding in softer snow.*

vertically on a backpack (Photo-6-11). If you plan to carry your skis or board a lot, buy a backpack with straps specific for this purpose; it will save you time.

Sometimes for fast transitions it makes sense to simply carry your skis in your hands, such as over a gentle slope along a flat ridge or up a steep but short section with low risk of falling. Again, use one or two straps to bind your skis and any unused ski poles into an easy-to-carry bundle. You can carry skis over your shoulder or a board under your arm, so long as there is no need for self-arresting.

In powdery snow conditions with solid snow underneath for kicking steps, snowboarders can hold the board by the bindings (perpendicular to the fall line) with the top sheet facing you and the edge slicing into the snow (Photo 6-12). Skiers can place the bases together and hold the skis so that the edges dig in (Photo 6-13). In firmer snow you will need to hit your skis against the snow with greater force so they have some snow to push against. Another option is to self-belay yourself by jabbing the tail of one ski in the snow (while keeping the other one on your back). When you want to take a rest, push the edges into the snow so your boards do not slide away. When the snow is firm, rest your knees against the snow and lay your boards across them or use your knees to push the boards against the slope.

## CONSIDERATIONS FOR SKIERS

Skis designed for mountaineering applications will have a straight tail, which allows you to push the ski into the snow. This allows your skis to act as handholds, to be safely stored so they do not slide away, to be used as an anchor, and to be used like a stake for securing a tent. Twin tip skis and even some models with a rise will fail at these tasks because the curved tails will not easily penetrate the snow.

### Kicking steps with ski boots and crampons

Climbing in alpine or telemark boots has advantages and disadvantages. Alpine ski boots come in two basic varieties, those designed for the ski area and those with the backcountry in mind. This second variety is referred to as alpine touring (AT) boots. AT boots perform better for climbing because they weigh less, have a Vibram sole which provides better traction, and allow much greater flex in the ankle when worn in "walk" mode which makes climbing easier.

Telemark boots share a similar design, but the distinction between boots for touring and boots for steep slopes is less distinct. Touring boots are typically lighter, shorter, and less rigid. Boots for more difficult skiing look more like alpine ski boots.

The basic procedure for kicking steps in ski boots is exactly the same as when wearing leather boots. Because they are so stiff, front-pointing is easy and less tiring, but this stiffness prevents you from using the walking technique to gain much elevation. Instead, sidestep or duck walk on lower angle slopes. Walking and scrambling on rock is less graceful so edging is your only real option when climbing rocks. Because ski boots have welts, crampons with heel and toe bails will be most secure. Wearing crampons with ski boots requires you to modify your technique. Front-pointing is also easy while wearing crampons, but even with a rigid ankle it is still possible to have your heels elevated. A flat-footed (French) technique is very difficult so you will need to rely on edging more often. In softer snow, do this by kicking the edge of your boot into the slope and let the crampons dig out a bit of a platform. In firm snow, the rigidity of your boot will allow you to stand with only your uphill points penetrating the snow. As discussed earlier, edging on ice is dangerous.

If you plan on wearing your ski boots for difficult snow, ice, and rock routes, go to a safe place to improve your technique. Find some local boulders or set up a top rope. Do not just practice on the steep faces either; these may sometimes be easier than lower-angle areas because ski boots edge well. Try climbing some slabby and blocky routes that require you to use a smearing technique when wearing leather boots or rock shoes.

*Photo 6-15. Kick steps with your feet and use the skis as handholds. Finish climbing over the lip by removing one of your skis, jabbing it into the snow, and using it as a handhold while you remove the other ski and climb over the lip. (Photo by Chris Blees)*

*Photo 6-14. To use your skis as ladders, first drive the tails into the slope as high above your head as possible. (Photo by Chris Blees)*

### Using skis to assist the ascent over a bulge

If you encounter a steep section of snow, stab the tails of your skis into the slope (so long as your skis have straight tails) and mantle up on them. (See Photos 6-14 and 6-15.) If the steep section extends for more than a body length, repeat these steps over and over. The snow must be soft enough for you to kick steps and to stab your tails in. If the snow is too firm, you should probably put your skis on your pack and use an ice ax.

### Putting on and taking off skis on a steep slope

When the ascent is over and you are ready to descend, it is critical to safely attach your boots to your skis. The safest and easiest solution is to start from a flat spot where you can clip in to the bindings without worrying about falling or losing equipment.

If you cannot find a flat spot, chop out a small platform. In soft snow you can do this with your feet. Face the slope while using your ax, skis, or poles for balance; then kick your toes into the slope while moving side to side (Photo 6-16). If the snow is too firm, use your ax. Make the platform slightly longer and wider than your skis. The safest platform will also angle slightly into the slope, which will help prevent your skis from sliding off it.

### Putting your skis on

Kicking out a platform with your ski boots is often not necessary. Skis with straight tails give you the option of jabbing the skis into the snow and getting into your bindings one at a time. (See Photo 6-17—6-20.) To do this, stick your poles in the snow and jab your second ski deep into the snow to act as a handhold. Jab the tail of the downhill ski into the snow at a slightly raised angle. This prevents the ski from sliding out of its pocket. Clean any snow from your boots so

*Photo 6-16. Kicking out a platform to put on skis. (Hint: Always make it larger than you think it needs to be.)*

Photo 6-17. The first step for getting into your bindings on a steep slope is to push the tail of your downhill ski into the snow.

Photo 6-18. Next, kick the toe of your uphill foot into the snow below your ski and click into your binding. Use your other ski or your ski poles for support.

Photo 6-19. Now push the tail of your uphill ski into the slope so it won't slide away.

Photo 6-20. Lastly, click into your uphill ski's binding.

*Photo 6-21. When clicking out of your skis, click out of the uphill ski first.*

*Photo 6-22. Stepping below your other ski while you click out of your binding helps prevent the ski from sliding away.*

that your bindings engage correctly. Step below the ski with your uphill leg and click your downhill leg into the binding; make sure it is locked in before you step up on it. Now jab the tail of the uphill ski into the slope at an angle and hold onto your ski poles while you get into your binding.

### Taking skis off

Not every ski run ends at a big flat spot. You may have to stop and remove your skis in the middle of a slope because the terrain below is too difficult, or because rocks or a cliff block your descent.

Removing your skis on a steep slope is similar to putting them on but in reverse order. Rule number one: Do not drop them! Try to stomp out a platform that you can stand on. If the snow is too firm to stomp flat, take your skis off while edging on the slope. (See Photos 6-21 and 6-22.) Stab your ski poles (with the grips facing down) deep into the snow above you for a handhold. Now bend down and click your uphill boot out of the binding with your hand. Jab your uphill ski into the snow at a height that allows you to still grab the ski. Now step below the other ski with your uphill foot. Reach down again and remove your ski.

### Self-arresting on skis

Self-arresting while wearing skis is difficult for several reasons, including that the edges of your skis are likely to catch on the snow as you are sliding, and flip you headfirst down the slope. Falls on steep terrain while wearing skis are often uncontrollable cartwheels. If you have your skis on when you fall, your feet are most likely to be parallel to the slope and you will have to rely on your poles for self-arresting. If skiing with a self-arrest-grip pole, hold your pole exactly as you would an ice ax. Placing your hand over the top of the head is more secure than merely grabbing the grip. (See Photo 1-5.) Grab the shaft of the pole with your other hand about two feet down.

## CONSIDERATIONS FOR SNOWBOARDERS

The split board has made a comeback in snowboarding. It allows snowboarders to leave the snowshoes behind and travel lighter. This is particularly important when kicking steps is involved. Having a snowboard, ski poles, and snowshoes on your pack gets cumbersome. Snowboarding with an ax in your hand can be dangerous. Riders only do this on slopes with severe consequences for a fall. A shorter ice ax is preferable.

### Kicking steps with snowboard boots and crampons

Snowboard boots come in two basic varieties, hard and soft. Hard boots resemble or are actually plastic mountaineering boots with a removable insulated liner. These boots are superior to soft boots for kicking steps. Most soft boots are not designed for climbing, and few have a Vibram sole. Kicking steps in these boots is more difficult than in stiff leather hiking boots. To accommodate this you could wear your hiking boots in the summer if you have a long approach on dry ground. In winter, riders usually wear soft boots for the climb. If you wear your boots tight, curl your toes when kicking steps to keep from "banging" your toes against the front of your boots. If kicking steps becomes difficult, wear crampons. Some crampons are designed for boots with a more rounded toe and heel. Recognizing when to wear crampons requires personal awareness and experience. Remember that baggy pants and crampons do not mix. Catching crampon points on your pants may cause you to fall.

### Putting your snowboard on

In softer snow you may be able to make a seat by plopping your butt down or by kicking a divot with your boots. Once you are seated, kick your heels into the snow to secure yourself. Jab your ax into the snow by your side so you can easily grab it. Put your front foot into the bindings and then kick the heel-side edge into the snow so that the board is secure. Finish by securing your back foot.

Use your ax to create a small platform if the snow is too firm. Make the platform slightly longer and wider than your board. Angle the platform slightly into the slope to prevent your board from sliding off.

### Taking off a snowboard

In soft snow, the easiest way to take off your snowboard is to sit on your butt and kick your heel-side edge into the snow. Take your back foot out first and kick your heel into the snow for security. Now lift your snowboard up and unclip your front foot while keeping a good grasp on your board.

On firm snow, removing your board is more difficult. Stopping on your toe side is easier and a better position to be in for removing your board. If you stop on your heel-side edge and rolling onto your toe-side edge seems unsafe, carefully remove your pack to retrieve your ax. If falling is a concern, your partner can retrieve your ax.

To remove your board when you are on your toe-side edge, unbuckle your rear foot first and then step down below your board. After you have kicked your foot into the slope, remove your front foot from the bindings. If you need the security of an ax, use the self-arrest position or use the self-belay technique to secure yourself.

### Self-arresting for snowboarders

Self-arresting on steep, firm snow while on a snowboard is challenging, but you should prepare by practicing in advance. Using your ax to stop yourself while on a snowboard varies depending on which edge is against the snow. If you are on your toe-side edge, fall into the self-arrest position. Grab the top of the head of your ax with one hand and grab the shaft near the spike with the other. Pull your arms in tight so the weight of your torso is over your ax. Turn your head away so your adze does not poke you in the face. Depending on the snow conditions and your speed, digging your edge into the snow may help slow you. If the snow is firm, digging your edge into the snow may cause you to flip over. On hard snow, it is best to have your knees against the slope and to lift your heels so your edge does not catch. If you are on your heel-side edge, slow down by holding the ax as you would for a seated glissade, but dig the pick into the snow.

# Chapter 7

*This mellow traverse above a lake is not what it seems. The snow is hanging over the lake and the edge of the lake is actually to the uphill side of the climber.*

# Hazards and How to Avoid Them

*"Good judgment comes from experience and experience comes from bad judgment."*

What the above quote does not say is that there must be a certain amount of reflection that occurs after a bad experience that keeps you from making the same mistake again and again. Only through discipline will you keep from repeating bad decisions. First of all, keep yourself from becoming a casualty of natural selection when you are just learning by seeking instruction and finding a qualified mentor. Do not spend your time with someone if they can not explain why they are doing something a certain way. Just because they can climb well does not mean they know how to do it safely or teach you how to do it. Teaching is a discipline all to itself.

Practice your skills at home and in the field. Get in shape. The less physically tired you are on a climb, the better your chances of being able to look around, make clear decisions, and act on them. Running on flat ground or using the Stairmaster is no substitution for hiking steep terrain with a pack on.

Be disciplined in decision making. Knowing it is time to remove your crampons is one thing; stopping to do it is another. Experienced climbers use what is called an expedition mentality. This means considering how your actions affect not only you but also the group. Risks you might be willing to take on a day hike are different from those on a big trip with a group.

Consider the mantra "Speed is safety." Before blindly incorporating this idea into your climbing, consider whether you are proficient enough in your skills to attempt them more rapidly. The 2007 edition of *Accidents in North American Mountaineering* posed important questions regarding the relationship between speed and safety: "Do we need to compromise safety for speed?

## THE CONSCIOUS COMPETENCE MATRIX

The Conscious Competence Matrix is a model for helping people identify their level of proficiency. Read the following four levels and see where you would place yourself.

### Unconscious Incompetence (You Don't Know that You Don't Know)

Ignorance is bliss. At this level you are unaware of the hazards or necessary skills for climbing. You lack the skills as well. You are likely to exceed your abilities and get in trouble.

### Conscious Incompetence (You Know that You Don't Know)

Through experience you have become aware of when your skills do not match the level required to proceed safely. If your ego will allow, accept that other people may be more competent than you, and that instruction would be helpful. You may spend years at this level. (This isn't a bad thing. Although I have spent a lot time on glaciers and have taken graduate geology courses devoted to them, I am extra cautious when the glacial terrain gets complex.)

### Conscious Competence (You Know that You Know)

You are acquiring new skills and experiences. You have awareness of how well your skill level fits the terrain you are climbing. You have not yet reached mastery because your skills have yet to reach an "automatic" level. You keep learning and your confidence increases.

### Unconscious Competence (You Don't Know that You Know, You Just Do It)

This is what you have been training for. You make safe decisions without having to think about it.

But wait! You have only reached mastery of the medium for which you have been training. As soon as you move into a new environment you may move right back into Unconscious Incompetence. Because you have reached mastery of other skills you will be more likely to recognize your incompetence in new situations.

*Photo 7-1. A rock that has fallen onto the slope tends to melt the snow around it forming a depression.*

*Photo 7-2. A rock protruding from the snow that is part of a larger feature tends to extend above the snow surface.*

What are the consequences of compromising safety?" Consider these ideas long and hard the next time you think it is time to start moving faster.

Read books to learn from other people's mistakes. Of course reading too many books, such as *Touching the Void,* by Joe Simpson, might make you decide that climbing is too dangerous.

## ELEPHANT TRAPS

Elephant traps is the colorful name for voids under the snow that form around boulders and the edges of mountains (Figure 7-1). When rocks and trees heat in the sun they radiate heat. Snow located near exposed rocks and trees melts out faster, causing large voids to develop under the snow surface. Tree wells are similar, except tree wells are usually visible. Near large rock outcrops, these hidden holes can extend more than 10 feet down. Near small boulders, melted out zones can extend a couple feet. Approach exposed rocks cautiously, and probe the snow with an ax or ski pole. Negotiate the transition between snow and a boulder field or rock buttress by avoiding the melt out zone or by taking a large step or leaping across.

It takes practice to evaluate whether an exposed rock at the snow surface is the edge of an elephant trap or just a natural depression formed by a rock that has fallen on the slope. Notice how the fallen rock in Photo 7-1 has melted snow around it, forming a depression. The rock in Photo 7-2

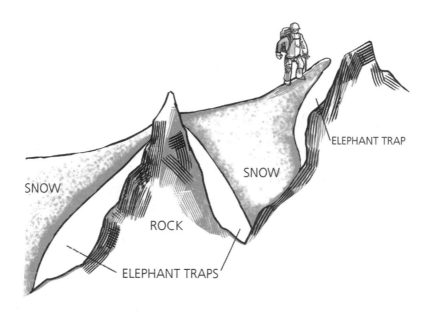

*Figure 7-1. Elephant traps are dangerous voids that can form near rock outcrops and even small boulders because rocks radiate heat and melt the surrounding snow.*

is part of a much larger feature and sticks out above the snow. Notice the icy ring surrounding this potential elephant trap.

## SNOW GATORS

Just like real alligators, snow gators can be dangerous to step on or near. Snow gators are logs just under the snow surface and the small cavity around them. These smooth,

wet, dead logs are very slippery. If you step just before or just after the log, you may punch through the snow and into a melted void surrounding the log, injuring your leg. Snow gators are most dangerous in the afternoon when the snow is getting soft, but if the snow layer above them is thin they can strike at any time of day. Keep an eye out for the ends of logs protruding from the snow. Choose a path that keeps you away from these.

## AVALANCHES

Climbing and descending on snow inevitably exposes you to the type of terrain where avalanches occur. The best season for climbing snow is usually summertime, when the snow is in a melt-freeze cycle, the snow is firm enough for you to kick steps, and the avalanche danger is low. At this point in the year new snow accumulation has generally ended and individual snow grains have metamorphosed to a spherical shape with maximum contact between them. During the day, sunlight and rocks warm the snow, allowing liquid water to percolate through the snowpack; at night, if temperatures drop below freezing the snow freezes. As the summer progresses, the chances of an avalanche occurring decrease, but so does your chance of finding snow.

This book is not a substitute for proper instruction in avalanche safety. There are many excellent books dedicated entirely to the subject of avalanches. Read one or two of those and take a course in avalanche safety. In the meantime, the following text will introduce you to some concepts that most relate to this book.

### PLAN AHEAD AND BE PREPARED

Take an avalanche and first-aid course; they are worthwhile investments. If you plan to travel in the mountains when avalanches are possible, it is important to bring and know how to use a shovel, probe, avalanche beacon, slope meter (inclinometer),

and first-aid kit. Remember to wear your avalanche beacon close to your body, not stored in a pocket or in your pack; an avalanche could tear your pack or coat from you and you want the beacon to be with you if you are buried. Also be sure your beacon is turned to "transmit" as you venture into avalanche territory.

Every brand of beacon is different; buy a beacon and learn to use it by practicing with it regularly. Get together with friends to practice your skills by stomping out a large area of snow in a safe location. Disturbing a large area of snow allows your friends to bury their beacons (while your back is turned), but not have it obvious where they have put them. Wrap buried beacons in padding and place them in a backpack to keep them dry and to prevent damage from probes and shovels. Make sure they are turned to transmit or they may be lost until spring. Time each other. Some friendly competition is good motivation to encourage people to become proficient. Remember that your only chance of survival if you are buried will come from your friends at the scene of the avalanche.

Check the weather and your local avalanche information center to learn about the conditions in your area. Remember that these are generalizations and you may encounter different conditions. Choose the right time for your climb. Avalanches are most common during a storm and for the first 24 hours afterward. The snowpack will slowly stabilize after that. As mentioned above, summer is the best season for climbing snow, but early in the season climbers should be concerned about wet slab avalanches and point release sloughs, both of which occur more often in the afternoon. If you plan to climb slopes that could slide, get up early and climb and descend before the snow softens. This cannot be stressed enough: Start your climb long before the sun rises, especially if you are climbing on the south or east face of a peak.

## APPROACHING YOUR CLIMB

While approaching your objective, keep your eyes and ears open for hints and warnings from Mother Nature. While it may have been a few days since a snowstorm, if the winds have been strong, leeward slopes receive additional snow and may again be unstable. Look for plumes of snow on the peaks and ridges to indicate the wind direction. The snowpack will produce a "whumping" sound if you walk on an unstable section and a weak layer collapses under you. On slopes too gentle to slide, consider this a warning that instability exists. On steeper slopes, your presence may trigger an avalanche. Look for evidence of recent avalanche activity, including avalanche debris, clean streaks that indicate where an avalanche has slid, and scars (fracture lines or flanks) on the slopes defining where an avalanche has occurred. Inspect your route for cornices and scan the area for evidence of recent cornice failures. If you dig a snow pit, remember that you have only assessed the snow in one location; where you plan to climb or ride may have entirely different conditions.

## ROUTEFINDING SKILLS

Conditions for an avalanche include an unstable snowpack, steep terrain, and a trigger. Assessing the snowpack is outside the scope of this book, but one of the things to look for is a slab of cohesive snow with a weak layer underneath. A weak layer collapsing is what produces the "whumping" sound discussed above. Listen for a hollow sound as you kick steps in the snow or probe the snow to feel for these layers. The amount your boot penetrates into the snowpack will give you an idea how soft the snow is getting. A general guideline is that if your foot penetrates up to your shin, then the snow is becoming dangerously soft.

Avalanches most commonly occur on slope angles between 30 and 45 degrees when slabs develop and a trigger releases them. On lower-angle slopes the downward pull of gravity helps hold the snow in place. On slopes steeper than 45 degrees the downward pull of gravity acts to pull the snow down the slope (sluffs) before a slab can develop. This sluffing can easily produce enough force to knock you down.

Always carry a compass with an inclinometer so you do not have to guess the slope angle. On most models the compass housing must be rotated to a particular position so the inclinometer can function properly. This usually means lining up the East or West mark with the Read Bearing Here mark. Lay your ski pole or ax on the snow, parallel to the fall line, to "smooth"

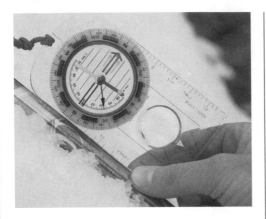

Photo 7-3. An inclinometer resting on a ski pole to measure slope angle. Ignore the magnetic needle and read the black needle that swings side to side as you tilt the compass. The slope in this photo is 45 degrees.

out any bumps. Set the edge of your slope meter on your pole to measure the angle of the slope (Photo 7-3). Estimating the angle of a slope far above you is nearly impossible. If you are at the base of a slope, you can look along the edge of the compass like a gun sight and use this line to point at the top of your route or the highest point you can see. This will only give you the average slope angle, but if the average is 35 degrees you can conclude that sections steeper than 35 degrees exist. When standing at the top of the slope, you can also use the inclinometer like a gun sight to measure the average angle of the slope below but also to measure a specific section if you can position yourself to look parallel to the surface. Notice how the skier in Photo 7-4

Photo 7-4. Stand so your compass looks along a line that intersects the top and bottom of the slope to get an average slope angle.

is standing far enough back so that the line of sight along the compass edge intersects the top of the slope. If you stand at the very edge and look down you are measuring the angle from your eye to the base of the slope; this will make the slope angle appear steeper. Remember that even if you are on a low-angle slope, you may be the trigger for a steeper slope above you.

The trigger for an avalanche may be you, your partner, a group of people above you, or a falling cornice. Avoid having climbers above you by being the first party on a route. If climbers are ahead of you, choose a different route or wait until they have moved to a location where their presence does not put you at risk. Travel one at a time through avalanche terrain and position yourself to see others while they are traveling.

Even though your objective may be to climb a steep slope, the following information is important because you can make small-scale routefinding decisions that reduce your chances of causing or getting caught in an avalanche.

- Expose only one person at a time to a potential avalanche slope. Examples of this include traversing across a steep slope and descending (skiing, snowboarding, glissading, and downclimbing) a steeper section. Remember that the first person down should be in a safe zone before additional members start descending. If an avalanche occurs, it should never catch more than one person.
- Avoid or minimize your exposure to avalanche terrain.

- Remember that ridges and low-angle slopes provide safer lines of travel.
- Avoid the leeward side of a ridge if the wind has loaded snow on that side.
- If the snow seems unsafe, travel on rock.
- Choose your route and resting locations out of the path of a potential avalanche.
- Stay near the edge if ascending or along the top of a slope if traversing to reduce the amount of snow above you if an avalanche occurs. Beware of the misconception that exposed rocks and trees act as safe zones. These objects heat up quickly and the snow around them may be weaker. Choose a happy medium between staying out of the center of a slope, yet not climbing too close to exposed rocks if the snow is unconsolidated.
- Observe the warnings that indicate signs of instability while climbing. These include free water in the snowpack (squeeze a handful of snow and if water drips out, the snow may be unstable), avalanches releasing near you, cornices breaking, and snow soft enough that you posthole above your calves in the main slope. Some postholing may be inevitable if you are near exposed rocks. Another sign of instability is rolling wheels of snow (Photo 7-5). Also called snow snails, these spirals of snow form in wet snow after a small piece of snow breaks free and rolls.
- Consider your entire route and plan accordingly. Different sides of the mountain will have different conditions at different times of day. Just because the snow is firm in a north-facing gully during your

*Photo 7-5. This snow snail released after a few inches of snowfall the night before and about one hour of direct sunlight the next morning.*

ascent does not mean the south face will be safe for descending. When the bottom of a gully is still in the shade, the top part could be heating up in the sun.

■ Look for escape routes in case your intended route turns out to be dangerous.

## CORNICES

A cornice is an overhanging block of snow shaped like a crashing wave, formed when snow blown from one side of a mountainous ridge accumulates on the other side.

Cornices present a problem when you are under them because they can break off and hit you or trigger an avalanche. They are dangerous to be on top of because they may break under your weight. Avoid being on top of the cornice on a ridge or crater rim by following these suggestions.

■ Traveling on rock is the safest way to ensure you are not on a cornice.

■ If you are not sure a cornice exists, approach the snow from the side to get perspective. When moving along a ridge, look ahead for cornices.

■ Be careful climbing the windward sides of ridges because cornices will not be visible (Figure 7-2). Top out on rock and approach the top of gullies cautiously.

It is critical to remember that there is no way to know whether a cornice is stable. There

Photo 7-6. top. A few cornices remain after most of the previous winter's snow has melted. Notice how far back the edge of the ridge is from the lip of the cornice. (Note the person on the ridge for scale.)

Figure 7-2. right. When you are on a snow-covered ridge where the bedrock is covered by snow, assessing where the dangerous travel zone is located will be difficult. When in doubt, travel more on the windward side of the ridge.

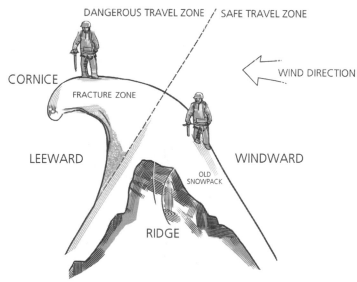

DANGEROUS TRAVEL ZONE / SAFE TRAVEL ZONE

WIND DIRECTION

CORNICE

FRACTURE ZONE

LEEWARD

WINDWARD

OLD SNOWPACK

RIDGE

are, however, some signs of definite instability, including water dripping from the lip of the cornice, other cornices failing nearby, and large voids between the cornice and the mountain where the snow has melted away.

If you cannot choose a cornice-free route, reduce the hazards of being below a cornice by staying out of its fall line. Use rock outcrops as protection or climb when the snow (including that of a cornice above) is frozen.

If there is no way to bypass a cornice, you may have to tunnel through. Be prepared to get wet and overheated. This should be your last resort because it is slow and you are weakening the cornice by digging into it.

Options for descending past a cornice include climbing or rappelling to the side of it, or cutting the cornice so that it falls first. Cutting the cornice should be a last resort because it may take a lot of time, your cut may not remove the entire cornice, and other climbers may be below you. Cutting a cornice usually entails two people on either end of the cornice sawing back and forth with a rope that has knots tied into it (like teeth on a saw). Never wrap the rope around your hands in case the cornice breaks and pulls your rope—and you with it.

## SNOWBRIDGES OVER CREEK CROSSINGS

In the spring, when water levels are high, snowbridges are a great way to cross creeks, but only if they hold. As summer approaches, bridges get thinner and the snow freezes less solidly each night. Keep your eyes open for the right places to cross.

Ask yourself if you need to cross. As you continue up valley, creeks get smaller and smaller. By the time you are above tree line, crossing to the other side of the valley may be a moot point.

Falling into freezing water on a cold morning can be serious. You may get swept downstream and pinned by another snowbridge or fallen tree; these can kill you. Follow these tips to help make your crossing as safe as possible:

- Cross where the snow is thicker and the distance across your creek is smallest.
- Consider the consequences if the bridge fails. It might be safer to cross a thinner bridge with a mellow stretch of open water below than a thicker bridge with rapids and obstructions below.
- Cross when the snow is frozen.
- Consider crawling on your hands and knees with branches under your hands to distribute your weight.
- Cross one at a time.

Snowbridges can be hazardous on your descent as well. When glissading lower down on a mountain, be careful you don't get funneled into a zone where the snow has been eroded from underneath by flowing water.

## ROCKFALL

Climbing steep snow slopes and gullies puts you below rock faces. The narrower the slope, the worse your chances are for getting out of the way. If you think, "It won't happen to me. The mountains look eternal," think again. The Rocky Mountains have been rising and eroding for nearly 70 million years. Mountains get smaller through almost imperceptible effects of erosion.

Predicting when rockfall will happen is impossible, but you can do a few things to keep yourself safer. The most common time of rockfall is after the rock has been exposed to sunlight. When water freezes, its volume increases by about 9 percent. This is why your full water bottle cracks when it freezes. During the day liquid water flows into the cracks between rocks. When the water freezes at night, it expands and separates the rocks. When the sun warms the rock the next day it melts the ice, breaking the "glue" holding loose rocks to the wall. The tricky thing is that the sun hits different rocks at different times of day: northeast- and east-facing rocks in the morning, south-facing rocks at noon, and west- and northwest-facing rocks in the afternoon. Rockfall happens at any time of day.

Pay attention to the fall line. On a slope that goes straight up the fall line, falling debris may travel the entire length of the route. Rocks that fall in a gully that is angled with respect to the fall line means debris is less likely to travel down the entire length of the slope. Steeper faces allow rocks to fall farther and faster.

Protect yourself by climbing early (even in the dark), taking a route that keeps you out of the fall line, and planning rest stops in protected areas. Also, wear a helmet and pack that you can hide under. Avoid the temptation to look up if you hear rocks coming. If rocks are falling, tuck your head

under your helmet and pack, get into the self-arrest position to give yourself a small vertical profile, or duck behind a rock if possible. If you dislodge a rock, always yell, "Rock!" to warn other climbers. Parties should cross a rockfall-prone slope one at a time. The person who is climbing should cross as fast as possible without looking up for falling rocks. Those who are not climbing should position themselves in a safe location where they can also see the slope above; they act as the eyes for the climber and yell instructions (e.g., "keep going," "get down!"). Lastly, never throw rocks off mountains. Climbers have been killed by these acts of stupidity.

## CREVASSES

Routefinding on a glacier requires an understanding of roped team travel, crevasse rescue, and how to avoid crevasses. Rope team travel and crevasse rescue are skills that require lots of experience to gain proficiency. Take a class or find expert instruction. A glacier is very complex. Predicting the location of crevasses requires much more than memorizing a basic diagram. A thorough understanding of glaciers should include consulting a textbook on the topic. Because crevasses may be covered by a bridge of snow from the previous winter, understanding how a glacier moves is critical to predicting where crevasses may exist and adjusting how your team travels.

Crevasses are fractures in the snow and ice at the surface of a glacier; deeper down the ice is less brittle and deforms instead of fracturing. Crevasses occur in places where the glacier is being stretched. A glacier actually flows, which means areas near the surface and at the center move faster than ice that is deeper or near the edges, similar to a river. Because ice and snow near the surface is brittle, cracks develop perpendicular to the stress. They can be a few inches or tens of feet wide. To avoid crevasses, all members of the rope team should be alert for signs of crevasses below (e.g., holes, cracks, or depressions that may be sagging bridges).

On the lower section of a glacier, where any snow from the previous year has melted, crevasses are obvious. When traveling on what is referred to as the "dry glacier," steel crampons are a must. High on the glacier where snowfall is typically largest, crevasses may be hidden because the snow from the previous year has formed large stable snowbridges across them. Snowbridges become thinner, weaker, and begin to sag as more of the previous year's snow melts. Bridges will be strongest when the snow is frozen. Snowbridges are thinnest and most dangerous just above the zone where any snow from the previous year has melted away and exposed the ice below.

To avoid accidents the rope team should try to travel perpendicular to crevasses so that only one person is exposed to each

## LEARNING FROM EXPERIENCE: LOST IN A WINTER STORM

*"If you bring bivouac equipment along, you will bivouac."*

—Yvon Chouinard

My most important mountain experience, by far, came soon after I started climbing. Eight of us were attempting a winter ascent of Mount Yale in Colorado. We had left most of our gear at a campsite below tree line. Even after it started snowing we kept hiking because we perceived our ridge as an obvious line of descent. We finally turned around because we were moving too slow to get to the summit and back to camp before dark. At some point we realized we were headed in the wrong direction. It was too dark to find our way back so we built a snow shelter. We spent about 14 hours in our shelter with only the clothes we had brought with us for the day. We passed the time digging out the doorway and doing calisthenics outside. We found our way out the next morning, unharmed. I did not realize it at the time, but knowing I could suffer through the night if necessary decreased my anxiety about climbing mountains. Our evening would have turned out very differently had we not made a proper shelter. Knowing how to dig a snow cave or construct a quincy can mean the difference between life or death.

crevasse at a time. If the edges of a crevasse are clearly defined, jumping or stepping over is safe. If you must cross a snowbridge, walk gently versus taking fast leaping steps. Probe with your ice ax, the grip end of a ski pole, or an avalanche probe to determine the location of a snowbridge. Skis and snowshoes distribute your weight, which can help reduce your chances of breaking through a snowbridge. Glissading down a glacier should generally be avoided.

## WHITEOUTS

A whiteout is when your visibility is dramatically reduced because you are in a very thick cloud or snowstorm. During whiteout conditions, climbers have walked off cliffs and lost their way. Expecting to follow your tracks back to camp (or finding your skis stashed in the valley) may be impossible. If getting caught in these conditions is a possibility, plan your route ahead of time and anticipate navigational errors by consulting a map and paying close attention when visibility is good.

### SNOW SHELTERS

Snow shelters for emergencies come in two basic varieties. The first is the snow cave which is created by finding an area of already consolidated snow (e.g., where wind has deposited the snow behind a large boulder) and digging your cave upward and into this feature. The second, the quincy, involves shoveling snow into a large pile while other members of the group work to harden the snow by continually walking over the growing pile. In places where the snow is powdery (e.g., the interior mountains of the United States in winter) this process is essential to force the snow grains to stick together. In places with wetter snow, the snow sticks together more readily. Once a large enough pile is created it is best to let the snow settle for an hour before you start digging your quincy. A snow shelter is probably the best refuge you can create if lost in a storm. Because of its insulating properties, a shelter made from snow will keep you much warmer than hiding under an overhang of rocks or even in a tent, especially if the shelter's doorway is lower than its inside platform. Remember to poke an air hole in the ceiling.

## THUNDERSTORMS

Afternoon thunderstorms are a major concern in the Rocky Mountains, especially in the summer. Because these storms are very isolated events (sometimes building in a single drainage), weather maps fail to predict them. These are a problem if you are climbing in a narrow gully because you may not see the thunderstorm building on the other side of the peak until it is too late.

It is not just the direct lightning strike that can get you. Electricity travels through the mountain and the water on it. Even if you are below the summit you could get a jolt of electricity that causes neurological damage or knocks you off balance. Even hiding under an overhang, while protecting you from the rain, may result in electrocution because the ground current may "jump" the gap that forms between the roof and the floor of the overhang.

If you have a good view you may be able to see the storm and track its movements. Another technique for tracking a storm is counting the number of seconds between a lightning strike and thunder associated with it. Lightning and thunder occur at the same time. Because light travels much faster than sound (186,000 miles per second versus about 1100 feet per second [about 1 mile every 5 seconds]) you see the flash of lightning and then wait for the sound of the thunder. For example, if you see a flash of lightning and count three seconds before the sound of thunder, it means the lightning occurred a little more than half a mile away. This in itself tells you the storm is very close, but if the timing for the next strike is only two seconds, the storm is moving toward you. Remember that lightning may be occurring within a cloud or between clouds, so a strike that appears half a mile away may be above you.

Avoid lightning and the cold wind and rain that come with it by learning about the local weather and what time storms are occurring. Start your climb early. In thunderstorm-prone ranges of the western United States, storms generally start as early as 11:00 in the morning and may continue past sunset. The only recommended place to be in the mountains during a thunderstorm is in a low area of large, evenly sized trees. Without a distinct high point nearby,

you are less likely to get struck. If you live in a thunderstorm-prone area buy a book or take a class to learn more about recognizing severe weather and what to do during a thunderstorm.

## SUNBURN

You are more prone to sunburn while climbing in the alpine because snow is a good reflector of ultraviolet light and because at high elevations less air exists above you to absorb harmful ultraviolet radiation. No, you are not closer to the sun. At 93 million miles away, 10,000 feet (about two miles) is insignificant.

While some consider "raccoon eyes" something to be desired, no one thinks "pizza face" looks good. Avoid sunburn and snow blindness (sunburn to your eyes) by wearing sunscreen, lip balm with sunscreen, sunglasses, and a wide-brimmed hat. If I am going to be on snow for many days I use tape to build a nose guard on my sunglasses because no amount of sunscreen seems to prevent me from burning.

## HYPOTHERMIA

A practical definition for hypothermia is being too cold to take care of yourself. Preventing hypothermia means staying dry, keeping out of the wind, and producing more heat than you lose but not so much that you sweat excessively. Dressing in layers (no cotton!) allows you to fine-tune your temperature. If your climbing partner is getting cold, address the heat gain and heat loss variables from Chapter 1 before he or she becomes too cold to eat and drink. Remember that it is easier to stay warm than to get warm, so put extra layers on before you start getting cold. Shivering generates heat but not as much as exercise does. If you are stuck in one spot during a storm, keep warm by doing exercises such as squats and lifting rocks.

## FROSTBITE

Frostbite occurs when your tissue freezes. Avoid frostbite by keeping your hands and gloves dry, and covering exposed skin. Avoid soaking your warmest gloves by wearing either thin liners or uninsulated shell gloves when the temperature allows. Warm your cold hands by putting them on

your belly. If your feet are on the verge of frostbite, put them on your partner's belly. For cold places like Alaska or the Rocky Mountains in winter, insulate the top of your ax by folding a four-inch square of ensolite over the top of the head and taping the ends together.

## TRENCH FOOT

Trench foot (immersion foot) is a very painful, potentially debilitating non-freezing injury usually affecting feet when they are cold and wet for prolonged periods. It is unlikely you will develop this problem during a single day's outing, but it has happened. More commonly, exposure to cold wet conditions for many days during which your feet are unable to dry is the recipe for trench foot. Prevent trench foot by wearing waterproof boots, wearing gaiters to keep

### LEARNING FROM EXPERIENCE: DON'T RELY ON A TRAIL OF BREAD CRUMBS...AND IF YOU FIND ONE, STAY ON IT

During an attempt on California's Mount Shasta years ago my partner, Dan, and I were climbing both sides of a ridge when rocky outcrops forced us off the crest. Our fairytale mistake came later in the day as we descended in a storm. Like Hansel and Gretel and their trail of bread crumbs, we thought we would follow our trail of footprints in the snow along the ridge, but we discovered that our tracks had been erased by the snow and strong afternoon winds. After going around the wrong side of a spire, we ended up descending off the ridge. Lesson number two came after we found our tracks in the snow again much lower down. I convinced Dan to take a "shortcut" through some untracked snow and to rejoin our footprints lower down. We never saw our footprints again. After hours of wandering through the forest in the dark we found an old ski track...and followed it out! Conclusion: when we found our tracks in the snow near tree line, we should have stayed with them.

the snow out, and making sure your feet become dry and warm at least once a day.

## PLAN YOUR DAY TO AVOID HAZARDS

There are many things to keep in mind when planning your day. It may help to make a list until it becomes second nature. Safety, of course, should always be first and foremost on your mind. Lightning, parties above you, avalanches, postholing, and falling cornices are all things to avoid. Plan your climb based on where you want to be in the afternoon when the snow is getting soft and the thunderstorms are building, and work backward from there. For this example, assume you need to be off the peak and back down to tree line by one o'clock. Make a realistic estimation of how long different activities will take. Following is an example:

- 1.5 hours: Descending from the summit to tree line
- 30 minutes on the summit to eat and rest
- 3 hours: Climbing your route
- 3 hours: The approach from the car to where the route begins
- 1.5 hours: Drive to the trailhead
- 30 minutes to get out of bed, get dressed, and pack a snack

Total time needed from the time you wake up until you summit and get down to the safe zone in case of lightning and avalanches: 10 hours. Therefore, 3:00 AM is your wake-up time if you have made an accurate estimate of your day. When in doubt, wake up earlier. It is always better to be the first party on the route and to get back down while the snow is still good.

# Appendix: Teaching a Snow Travel 101 Class

There are two basic approaches to teaching others about climbing snow. In the first model, outlined below, students are taken through an entire introductory progression. This method allows you to monitor every student to ensure everyone practices the skills correctly the first time; it also allows you to address any potential bad habits right away.

A second model involves demonstrating a skills progression, then setting students free to practice them at their own speed. This model is great for fast learners who may lack patience or for those who need to experience the limitations of their abilities before they are open to further instruction. There are drawbacks to this style, however. First, demonstrating many different concepts and expecting students to grasp them all is a tall order. Overwhelmed participants may quickly lose enthusiasm for the topic. Second, when students are not receiving individual attention, they are more likely to form bad habits.

If you are lucky enough to have a job that involves taking people into the high country where the participants will be traveling on snowy terrain with an ice ax—or you just want to teach friends—the following lesson plan provides an introductory progression of skills to get you moving on low-angle snow.

## AN INTRODUCTORY PROGRESSION

Set yourself and your participants up for success by making sure your basic needs (e.g., food, water, warmth, and physical and emotional safety) are taken care of. If your

*An ideal location for an introduction to snow climbing*

participants are distracted by being cold, an impending thunderstorm, or the thought of climbing the steep mountain in front of them, they will not be focused on your lesson.

Consider starting your lesson with a discussion around the fears your group has related to this activity. Some common fears include getting impaled on the ice ax, falling and not stopping, fear of heights, and fear of failure. Remind students that you will teach the basic skills on a low-angle slope first and only when people are ready will you move on to new challenges. You might point to some routes that the group will be able to climb as well as routes you will avoid.

Depending on your level of comfort, proficiency, the weather, and the snow conditions, this progression can be completed in a couple hours or a couple days. Remember that learning should be fun! If the students have had enough "training" for the day, choose an objective (e.g., a small summit or pass) they can climb at their skill level to give them a sense of accomplishment.

1. Find a wide open slope without rocks. The slope should begin as a gentle incline before slowly increasing in steepness. Depending upon the temperature and the firmness of the snow, the sun or the shade may be preferable.

2. Prepare to get wet. Have students dress in waterproof pants and jackets, gloves, and helmets.

3. Walk using *pied marché* (walking flat-footed with toes forward) toward the slope until their feet begin to slip. Leave packs and axes in the snow at this high point. Start with participants carrying their ice axes correctly for nontechnical terrain.

   Without your ice ax, but wearing helmets, demonstrate kicking steps while beginning to gain some altitude. Practice sidestepping (including changing directions), the duck step, and front-pointing.

4. Climb high enough to easily slide if you fall, but not so steep that your students get worried.

5. Demonstrate the ideal self-arrest position without an ice ax. When you stand up, kick your feet into the snow to create a stable platform to stand in.

6. Demonstrate and have students practice self-arresting by sliding downhill in the three basic positions. (See Chapter 5.) Make sure they practice rolling to both sides. If the snow is not very conducive to sliding, have

*A group of friends make the most of the dwindling summer snowpack.*

students slide down the same path each time so it becomes easier to slide on. Turn your workshop into an active mini-climb by continually climbing higher than your previous high point before practicing a new self-arrest technique. Make sure participants slide one at a time and receive positive and constructive feedback after each attempt. Have students practice the following fall scenarios: back against the snow and feet downhill, chest against the snow and head downhill, and back against the snow and head downhill.

7. Have students practice self-arresting without an ice ax on steeper slopes and firmer snow until they are proficient and ready to progress.

8. When students have demonstrated proficiency, have students practice the plunge step and seated glissade back to your stashed equipment.

9. With your ice ax and helmet, demonstrate the ideal self-arrest position.

10. Demonstrate and have everyone practice the same techniques and progression as outlined in the previous steps for going up and down without an ice ax. For lower-angle slopes, students should only need the self-arrest grip or cane grip, and the self-belay techniques with their ax. Avoid giving your students too many different skills to work on all at once.

*Note:* While it seems as if much of your time has been spent teaching self-arresting, your goal is to produce competent climbers not people who can just self-arrest well! Knowing how to self-arrest is essential, especially for beginners on low angle slopes. But good risk management comes from training people to climb with good technique. If you are really worried about your inexperienced participants or friends taking a fall and needing to self-arrest to prevent injury, use a rope and give them a belay.

Many outdoor organizations teach their students to hold their axes using the self-arrest grip instead of the cane grip. The advantage to this is that if your participants will have limited instruction and practice climbing on snow, they may have a better chance of self-arresting if they fall. If students fall while holding the ax in the cane grip, they may fail to self-arrest effectively.

If you are teaching friends, clients, or students who will be moving over steep snow, it is essential to include some daggering techniques (low and high dagger and the self-arrest position, for example) and the single overhead swing in your lesson plan. Remember that climbing up is typically easier than climbing down. Choose your early climbing objectives wisely; look for objectives that have an easier line of descent.

# Glossary

**albedo.** The percentage of light that a surface reflects in relation to how much light the surface receives.

**alpine ice.** Ice that has formed from repeated melt-freeze cycles of snow.

**alpine touring (AT) boots.** A modified alpine skiing boot designed to perform better climbing uphill than traditional alpine ski boots.

**avalanche beacon.** A device that transmits and receives a radio signal to allow a buried climber to be found by others wearing a beacon. Also called a *transceiver*.

**avalanche probe.** A collapsible aluminum cylinder used to probe for a person buried in an avalanche.

**bergschrund.** The highest crevasse that separates a glacier from the semi-permanent snow at the head of a cirque or glacial valley.

**boot skiing.** Deliberately sliding down a slope, using your feet as skis on the surface of the snow while standing upright. Also known as the *standing glissade*.

**cairn.** A pile of rocks constructed by humans to mark a route or location.

**Camelbak.** A brand name of a water bladder that is stored in a pack and has a hose to allow the user easy access to water.

**cane grip.** A way of holding an ice ax like it is a cane, with the heel of your hand on the adze. Also known as *piolet canne*.

**clip-in point.** A location on an anchor, ice ax, or harness where a carabiner that will hold weight can be clipped.

**combination technique.** Front-pointing with one foot and kicking the inside edge against the snow with the other foot. Also known as the *American technique, three o'clock position*, and *pied troisième*.

**concave.** Curved inward, as opposed to being convex (curving outward).

**conduction.** The transfer of heat through direct contact between materials.

**Conscious Competence Matrix.** A learning model that describes a progression from incompetence to competence.

**convection.** The enhanced conduction of heat by a fluid (e.g., air or water) moving over a surface.

**cornice.** An overhang of snow that forms when snow grains are blown over a ridge and stick together on the leeward side.

**corn snow.** Large, rounded snow/ice grains that form after many melt-freeze cycles. Corn snow freezes overnight, then softens in the sun.

**couloir.** A gully or other narrow feature on a mountain; it frequently retains snow and ice.

**crampons.** Plates of metal with spikes (called points) that point down and outward. They are attached to boots to make climbing firm snow and ice easier.

**crevasse.** A crack that forms in the uppermost, brittle snow and ice on a glacier.

**cutting steps.** Using the adze of the ax to chop a small platform to place your foot. Also known as *chopping steps.*

**daggering.** Term used to describe pushing the pick into the snow.

**dry glacier.** The lowest portion of a glacier where all the previous year's snow has melted and only glacial ice is exposed.

**duck step.** A method of walking up or down a slope with your toes pointed slightly outward. Also known as *pied en canard.*

**elephant trap.** A melted-out pocket, of any size, with snow covering it that has formed next to a rock or mountainside.

**evaporation.** The change from a liquid phase to a gas phase.

**fall line.** The path an object will take sliding down a slope.

**firn.** Snow that has lasted one year without melting, but has not yet turned to ice.

**French technique.** Name for a number of crampon techniques where the climber keeps the sole of their boot entirely against the snow or ice.

**front-pointing.** Kicking your toe straight in with or without crampons. Also known as the *German technique.*

**frostbite.** Tissue damage that occurs when human tissue freezes.

**gaiters.** Contoured cylinders of nylon that cover the top of boots and the lower leg. They prevent snow and debris from getting into a boot.

**glissade.** To descend snow in a seated or standing position.

**heel-n-side.** A combination technique for angling downward in which you use the side of your uphill foot and heel of your downhill foot to maintain traction.

**high dagger.** A technique for holding the ax with your thumb under the adze and your fingers over the top of the ax head and then pushing the pick into the snow above your head. Also known as *piolet poignard.*

**hypothermia.** Decrease in body core temperature.

**inclinometer.** Instrument used for measuring angles of the slope. Also called a *clinometer.*

**infrared (IR) light.** A type of electromagnetic radiation with a wavelength longer than red-colored light. It is given off by humans or other objects of a similar temperature.

**leeward side.** The side of a ridge or mountain that is protected from the wind.

**lip.** The edge of a natural feature that divides the low-angle portion from the steep portion. Also known as the *edge.*

**low dagger.** Holding the ice ax in cane grip and pushing the pick into the snow. Also known as *piolet panne.*

**melt-freeze cycle.** A daily cycle that occurs in snow that thaws during the day and refreezes again at night.

**moat.** The gap that exists between a glacier or snowfield and the bedrock of a mountain.

**névé.** Term used by climbers for snow that is firm or Styrofoam-like, which crampons penetrate well. Scientifically, *firn* and *névé* are the same.

*pied.* The French term for "foot."

*piolet.* The French term for "ice ax."

*piolet ancre.* A technique that combines the single overhead swing with the self-arrest position and the low dagger.

*piolet manche.* Gripping the shaft of the ax just below its head and pushing the pick into the snow.

*piolet ramasse.* Holding the head of your ax in your downhill hand (using the cane grip) while holding the shaft near the spike with your uphill hand and pushing the spike into the snow to provide balance.

*piolet rampe.* A technique for descending firm snow and ice by swinging the pick into the snow and walking straight downslope while pulling up on the ax to maintain balance.

*piolet traction.* When the single overhead swing is used with an ax in each hand.

**plunge step.** A technique for descending soft snow in which you plunge your heel into the snow to control speed and provide traction.

**postholing.** Walking in unconsolidated snow so that your foot plunges in up to your shin or deeper forming a deep narrow hole.

**protection.** The general term for pickets (in snow), ice screws (in ice), and stoppers and cams (in rock) that climbers use to secure themselves to the mountain.

**quincy.** A type of snow shelter made when snow is initially piled up and then a cave is dug into it.

**radiation.** Energy in the form of electromagnetic waves, called light (e.g., ultraviolet, visible, and infrared).

**rest step.** A technique for taking short breaks in which a hiker stops with legs straight and the weight of the body rests on the skeleton, not the muscles.

**runout.** The terrain below (into which you might slide or land if you fall).

**saddle.** Low spot on a ridge between two higher points.

**sastrugi.** Intricate patterns formed by the wind scouring the surface snow.

**self-arrest.** To stop yourself if you slide down a snow slope.

**self-arrest grip.** At alternative version of the cane grip, but the thumb goes under the adze and the pick points backward.

**self-arrest position.** Holding the ice ax diagonally across your chest with one hand on its head using the self-arrest grip while holding the bottom of the shaft with the other hand.

**self-belay.** Holding the ax in the stake grip but plunging the shaft deep enough into the snow to serve as an anchor and so hold the weight of the climber.

**sidestepping.** A technique for kicking steps with the edges of the boot in which you traverse or follow a diagonal path up or down a slope.

**single overhead swing.** Holding the ice ax at the base of the shaft and swinging the pick into the snow or ice.

**skinning.** Progressing uphill while wearing skis with skins attached.

**slab avalanche.** An avalanche that begins with the sliding of a cohesive block of snow (a slab) down the slope.

**sloughs.** The release of noncohesive snow from a point that spreads out or becomes wider as it continues downslope. Also known as a *sluff, point release,* or *loose snow avalanche.*

**snowbridge.** A mass of snow that extends over a creek, crevasse, etc.

**snow gator.** A log that is partially or entirely covered with snow, but has a melted out cavity surrounding it.

**stake grip.** Holding the head of your ax with one hand on the adze and the other over the pick.

**sun crust.** Hard crust of snow that forms when snow is melted by sunlight and refrozen.

**sun cup.** Depression in the snow caused by the differential erosion of the snow by sunlight or warm winds.

**surface hoar.** Feathery ice crystals that form on the surface of the snow after a cold, calm, clear, and humid night.

**talus.** Accumulation of angular rocks on a slope or flat surface.

**telemark boots.** A type of ski boot used with a free heel binding.

**topo map.** Map that uses contour lines to show elevation.

**transition zone.** Place where the terrain or snow changes characteristics. Accidents commonly occur in these.

**trench foot.** A non-freezing cold injury that causes tissue damage when feet are wet and cold for a prolonged time. Also known as *immersion foot.*

**ultraviolet (UV) light.** A type of electromagnetic radiation with a shorter wavelength than violet-colored light. This wavelength is typically responsible for sunburns.

**walking in-balance.** Climbing snow in a diagonal fashion where the climber stops and rests when the uphill leg is above and forward of the downhill leg.

**walking technique.** Ascending using the traction of your boots' soles to grip the snow. Also called *marché.*

**water ice.** Ice formed when liquid water freezes, e.g., a frozen waterfall.

**watermelon snow.** The nonscientific term for a type of algae found on snow that looks and smells like watermelon; it is *not* safe to ingest.

**wet snow avalanche.** Typically a slough avalanche of wet unconsolidated snow.

***whumphing.*** The sound associated with the collapsing of an unstable layer of snow; often signals an unstable snowpack.

**windward side.** The side of the mountain on which the wind blows.

# Resources

American Alpine Club. *Accidents in North American Mountaineering*. Golden, CO: American Alpine Club, 2012 (published annually).

Chouinard, Yvon. *Climbing Ice*. San Francisco: Sierra Club Books, 1982.

Eng, Ronald C., and The Mountaineers. *Mountaineering: The Freedom of the Hills,* 8th edition. Seattle: The Mountaineers Books, 2010.

Flint, Richard. *Glacial and Quaternary Geology*. Hoboken: John Wiley & Sons, Inc., 1971.

Fredston, Jill, and Doug Fesler. *Snow Sense: A Guide to Evaluating Snow Avalanche Hazard,* 5th edition. Anchorage: Alaska Mountain Safety Center, 2011.

Harmon, Will. *Leave No Trace: Minimum Impact Outdoor Recreation*. Guilford, CT: Falcon Publishing, 1997.

Houston, Mark, and Kathy Cosley. *Alpine Climbing: Techniques to Take You Higher*. Seattle: The Mountaineers Books, 2004.

Lowe, Jeff. *Ice World: Techniques and Experiences of Modern Ice Climbing*. Seattle: The Mountaineers Books, 1996.

McGivney, Annette. *Leave No Trace: A Guide to the New Wilderness Etiquette,* 2nd edition. Seattle: The Mountaineers Books, 2003.

Schimelpfenig, Tod, and Joan Safford. *NOLS Wilderness Medicine,* 4th edition. Mechanicsburg, PA: Stackpole Books, 2006.

Selters, Andy. *Glacier Travel & Crevasse Rescue*. 2nd edition, revised. Seattle: The Mountaineers Books, 2006.

Tremper, Bruce. *Staying Alive in Avalanche Terrain,* 2nd edition. Seattle: The Mountaineers Books, 2008.

Twight, Mark, and James Martin. *Extreme Alpinism: Climbing Light, High, and Fast*. Seattle: The Mountaineers Books, 1999.

Tyson, Andy, and Mike Clelland. *Glacier Mountaineering: An Illustrated Guide to Glacier Travel and Crevasse Rescue* (How to Climb Series). Guilford, CT: Falcon Publishing, 2009.

# Index

## About the Author

Mike Zawaski began climbing in 1990 and has made ascents of snowy peaks from Colorado to the West Coast and from Alaska down to Peru.

Mike fills many roles in science and outdoor education. His background in mountain safety includes six years of experience in mountain rescue (Yosemite Search & Rescue and Western State College Mountain Rescue Team), and he is in his twelfth year teaching for the Wilderness Medicine Institute of NOLS. He has seventeen years of experience instructing courses and training staff at the Colorado Outward Bound School, and he teaches college courses in astronomy, geology, and meteorology.

Mike runs the educational nonprofit the Observant Naturalist (www.observant naturalist.org), which provides scientifically accurate, fun, and experiential science education to teachers and the public.

THE MOUNTAINEERS, founded in 1906, is a nonprofit outdoor activity and conservation organization whose mission is "to explore, study, preserve, and enjoy the natural beauty of the outdoors...." Based in Seattle, Washington, it is now one of the largest such organizations in the United States, with seven branches throughout Washington State.

The Mountaineers sponsors both classes and year-round outdoor activities in the Pacific Northwest, which include hiking, mountain climbing, ski-touring, snowshoeing, bicycling, camping, canoeing and kayaking, nature study, sailing, and adventure travel. The Mountaineers' conservation division supports environmental causes through educational activities, sponsoring legislation, and presenting informational programs.

All activities are led by skilled, experienced volunteers, who are dedicated to promoting safe and responsible enjoyment and preservation of the outdoors.

If you would like to participate in these organized outdoor activities or programs, consider a membership in The Mountaineers. For information and an application, write or call The Mountaineers Program Center, 7700 Sand Point Way NE, Seattle, WA 98115-3996; phone 206-521-6001; visit www.mountaineers.org; or email info@mountaineers.org.

The Mountaineers Books, an active, nonprofit publishing program of The Mountaineers, produces guidebooks, instructional texts, historical works, natural history guides, and works on environmental conservation. All books produced by The Mountaineers Books fulfill the mission of The Mountaineers. Visit www.mountaineersbooks.org to find details about all our titles and the latest author events, as well as videos, web clips, links, and more!

The Mountaineers Books
1001 SW Klickitat Way, Suite 201
Seattle, WA 98134
800-553-4453
mbooks@mountaineersbooks.org

The Mountaineers Books is proud to be a corporate sponsor of The Leave No Trace Center for Outdoor Ethics, whose mission is to promote and inspire responsible outdoor recreation through education, research, and partnerships. The Leave No Trace program is focused specifically on human-powered (nonmotorized) recreation.

Leave No Trace strives to educate visitors about the nature of their recreational impacts and offers techniques to prevent and minimize such impacts. Leave No Trace is best understood as an educational and ethical program, not as a set of rules and regulations.

For more information, visit www.lnt.org, or call 800-332-4100.

# OTHER TITLES YOU MIGHT ENJOY FROM THE MOUNTAINEERS BOOKS

**Staying Alive in Avalanche Terrain**
2nd edition
*Bruce Tremper*
Accessible and engaging manual to
keep you safe in avalanche country

**Backcountry Skiing:
Skills for Ski Touring and
Ski Mountaineering**
*Martin Volken, Scott Schell,
and Margaret Wheeler*
The most up-to-date resource
available for backcountry skiers

**Glacier Travel and Crevasse Rescue**
2nd revised edition
*Andy Selters*
How to travel safely on glaciers—including
what to do when it goes awry

**Snowboarding: Learning to Ride
from All-Mountain to Park and Pipe**
*Liam Gallagher*
Covers everything from basics
about gear to mastering
air-to-fakies

**Backcountry Ski & Snowboard
Routes: Oregon**
*Christopher Van Tilberg*
95 fabulous snow routes throughout
Oregon—plus a few in California
and Washington

**50 Classic Backcountry Ski and
Snowboard Routes in California**
*Paul Richins, Jr.*
Classic descents and backcountry
routes in California

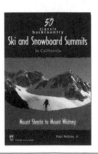

**The Mountaineers Books has more than
500 outdoor recreation titles in print.**
Visit www.mountaineersbooks.org for details.